While the Windmill Watched

Jackie Pfeiffer, age five

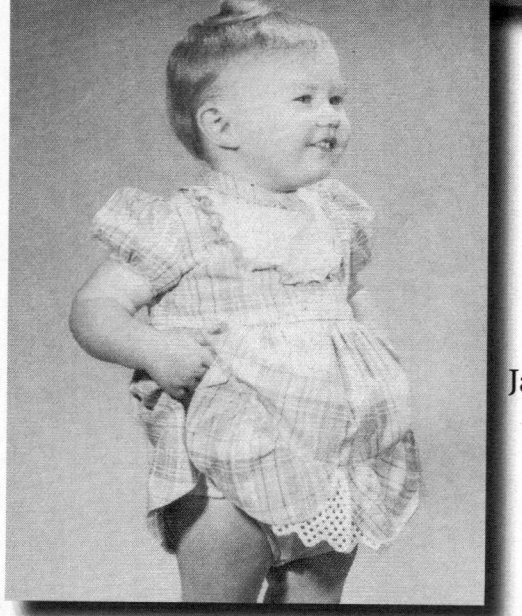

Janine Pfeiffer, age two

While the Windmill Watched

A Slice of Rural America
in the 1950s

Jackie Pfeiffer McGregor
Janine Pfeiffer Knop

While the Windmill Watched: A Slice of Rural America in the 1950s.

Copyright 2021 by Jackie Pfeiffer McGregor and Janine Pfeiffer Knop

Self-published

Printing by Bookmobile, Inc.

First Printing, April 2021. Second Printing June 2021.

ISBN 978-0-578-87528-6

Printed in the U.S.A.

Editor & Interior Book Design: Victoria Tirrel, ConsultVictoria.com
Cover Design & Photo Preparation: Joanie Christian, Joanie Christian Photography
Cover Photos: Background, David S. and Bevin Dvorak; windmill silhouette, Jim Puppe; girls silhouette, Joanie Christian
Interior Photos: Authors; except pages 28, 60, and 68 provided by Marlys Neugebauer Frandsen; and page 160, by Bill Koch, North Dakota Highway Department

Visit
WhiletheWindmillWatched.com
to order and for more information.

With everlasting love,
this collection of rural history
is dedicated to our parents,
Jack and Eudora Pfeiffer,
and the community of
Menoken, North Dakota.

The ability to record our recollections
on these pages would have been
difficult without the teaching mastery
of Mrs. Violette Arntz,
our grade-school teacher
at Menoken School.

We've shared many secrets,
  the same Mom and Dad.
We've shared lots of good times,
  Don't think of the bad.
Our memories we'll cherish
  with love without end.
I'm glad you're my sister.
  I'm glad you're my friend.

*From a hand-worked
counted cross-stitch piece
made especially for Janine
by Jackie, July 3, 1988*

Contents

Acknowledgments	ix
The Storytellers	xi
MEET THE PFEIFFERS	1
THE MENOKEN COMMUNITY	19
Chapter 1: Menoken School	23
Chapter 2: Community Challenges and Progress	49
Chapter 3: The Churches	59
Chapter 4: Menoken at Play	67
Chapter 5: Clubs	75
Chapter 6: Civic Life	99
LIFE ON THE PFEIFFER FARM	107
Chapter 7: The Animals	111
Chapter 8: The Equipment	145
Chapter 9: The Weather	153
Chapter 10: The Chores	165
Chapter 11: Preserving the Bounty	171

GROWING UP PFEIFFER ... 179
Chapter 12: The Sisters at Play ... 181
Chapter 13: Always Time for Beauty ... 187
Chapter 14: Days We'll Never Forget ... 199
Chapter 15: Lessons in Life and Art ... 227
Chapter 16: Our Last Words ... 243

AS WE PART ... 245
RECIPES ... 253

About the Authors ... 269

Acknowledgements

OUR ABUNDANT THANKS go to...

Almighty God who formed us into the authors we have become; we trusted Him for words, and He provided

Victoria Albertson of UPS Store #4352, Colville, Washington, for her photo scanning expertise

Joanie Christian Photography, Colville, Washington, for creating an attractive, meaningful cover design

Helen Danielson, friend and supporter

David S. and Bevin Dvorak, Park River, North Dakota, for sharing their masterful photographic glimpse of the North Dakota sky featured on the cover

Doug Goehring, North Dakota Agriculture Commissioner (and grandson of Dad's best friend, Howard Goehring), for reading the book and providing an endorsement

Mike Heilman, Burleigh County Superintendent of Schools, for providing a copy of the Y.C.L. Song

Fred Knop, loving, patient, supportive husband

Bob McGregor, loving, patient, supportive husband

Menoken neighbors Maureen Dance Kershaw, Linda Ehlers Schwengler, JoAnn Goehring Schrenk, Judy Goehring Miller, Marlys Neugebauer Frandsen, Marge Lein Perkins, Janny Salter Bashus, and Patty Salter Ennen

North Dakota State University Bookstore staff for their willingness to manage online book sales

Jim Puppe, Fargo, North Dakota, author of *Dakota Attitude,* for encouragement and use of his windmill photograph

Katherine Satrom, president of Satrom Travel & Tour/ Direct Travel, Bismarck, North Dakota

Bill Thomas, director of radio at Prairie Public Broadcasting, for reading the book and providing an endorsement

Victoria Tirrel, editor, organizer extraordinaire, and unofficial third Pfeiffer sister

Andrew Zalasky, Hazel Creative Services, Ames, Iowa, for his skillful creation of our website

The Storytellers

WHILE THE WINDMILL WATCHED is told in four voices—Jackie, Janine, The Sisters together, and the Windmill that watched over our farm and the surrounding Menoken community.

For the benefit of you, the reader, we've created a visual system to identify each storyteller. We hope this helps make the transition from storyteller to storyteller seamless. Here is a key to the voices of *While the Windmill Watched*.

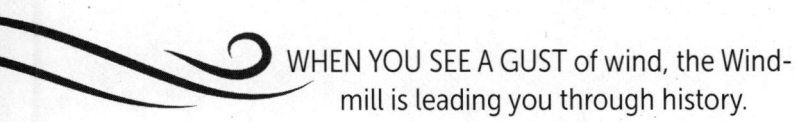 WHEN YOU SEE A GUST of wind, the Windmill is leading you through history.

 LIKE OUR PERSONALITIES, our identity markers are similar yet different.

 WHEN WE SPEAK in one voice, you will see us together, as we are here and on the cover.

With this system explained, we hand you our book. Enjoy your journey through this slice of American history during the 1950s.

—*The Sisters*

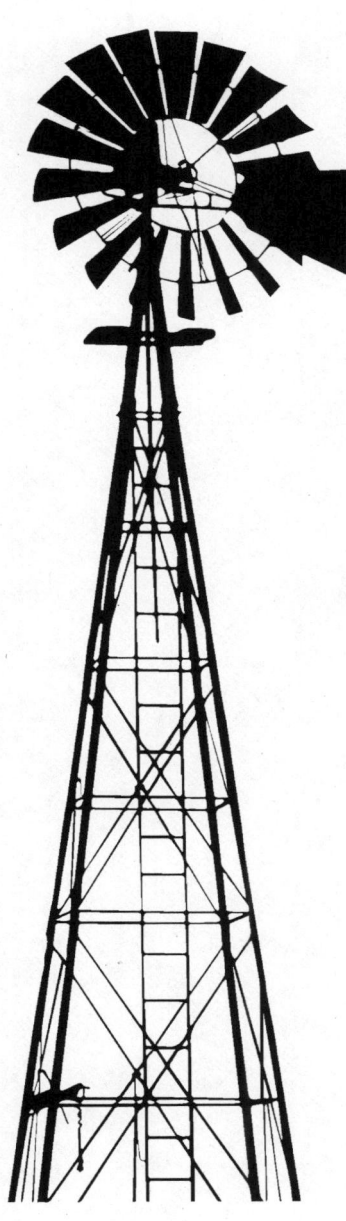

Meet the Pfeiffers

I AM THE WINDMILL, a towering intermediary between wind and underground water—thirst-quenching water. My coordinated mechanism draws life-giving water from the aquifer and stores this liquid within a circular, wooden stock tank for the refreshment of the livestock on the Pfeiffer farm.

Yet within this portrait of North Dakota history, I have an additional role. I am The Observer—The Observer of Time.

I stood as sentry over the land and people who awaken within these pages. Particularly, I observed the Pfeiffer sisters—Jackie and Janine, daughters of Jack and Eudora—as the years progressed. With a watchful eye, I caught sight of a recurrent theme in the metamorphosis of The Sisters' personalities. I found it to be true they were notably similar in integrity, honesty, morality, and work ethic, yet uniquely different in pursuits and experiences. It is hoped that you, reader, will also find this to be true as our tale unwinds.

Proof of the girls' unique, individual characters came to light on a summer day in 1954. The setting was my sturdy metal ladder.

For seven-year-old, adventurous Jackie, my rungs served as her forty-foot stairway to a world beyond the farm. As the breeze played with her long, blonde hair and moved the whirligig above her, she wondered what lay beyond the 360-degree view.

"Come on, come on up here! I can see the Capitol building from here!" Jackie implored four-year-old Janine.

"No, I'm not climbing any higher. I'm scared!" Chestnut-haired Janine had climbed a mere three rungs. Her security was with both feet planted on solid ground.

Their differences forecast their evolution into marriage and adulthood. Curiously adventuresome, Jackie moved to Alaska, The Last Frontier. Pragmatically adventuresome, Janine moved to the Iowa Midwest.

Seven decades hence, their unforgettable chronicles of history merge to tell the story of what happened on the North Dakota prairie while I, the Windmill, watched.

IN THE BEGINNING of this story, before the Pfeiffers were four or even a family of two, Justus (Jack/J.C.) Carroll Pfeiffer and Eudora Irene Wiese individually experienced a childhood history.

For instance, as with many children of first- or second-generation immigrants, which included Jack's parents, he spoke only the "mother tongue" of his family. This practice was not uncommon in the 1800s and early 1900s when America was known as the "melting pot" consisting of immigrants from around the world assimilating into one American society. In Jack's case, German was the predominant language spoken in the Pfeiffer home. When Jack began formal schooling in Goodrich, he learned the prevalent language of America—English.

Eudora and two of her four siblings shared the common mode of transportation for the time—a horse. All three Wiese children shared the responsibility of getting themselves to country school by riding on one horse with Eudora in charge of the reins. Then, after graduating from the eighth grade, Eudora moved into the town of Oakes. Because the Wiese farm was located ten miles from the nearest high school, she boarded with a family in Oakes in exchange for taking care of their children and doing light household chores during her out-of-school hours. Had she not made this move, a high school education would have been out of reach for her. The secretarial

Jack Pfeiffer, 1940

Eudora Pfeiffer, 1940

classes Eudora took and the high ranking she earned in her graduating class launched a professional career in office employment at the Dickey County Courthouse. A job offer at the State Capitol took her to Bismarck, where she and the handsome Jack Pfeiffer would soon meet, fall in love, and marry.

In 1978, Eudora briefly recorded some of their history prior to my observation for a Burleigh County history book:

> *The dry years of the 1930s drove many young people from the farms in search of gainful employment. Jack Pfeiffer and Eudora Wiese were two such people. They both went to Bismarck, but it wasn't until 1939 that they became acquainted through a mutual friend.*
>
> *Justus (Jack) was born April 18, 1912, to Charles and Justine Brost Pfeiffer on a farm near Goodrich, North Dakota. He graduated from Goodrich High School (May 27, 1932). He came to Bismarck in 1934. For two years while attending Capital Commercial College, he worked almost every waking moment. Starting at five in the morning, he was custodian for a bar, The State Recreation, then worked a full day in the office of Armour Creameries. From seven to midnight, he was a truck checker for Northern Hide and Fur Company.* [The daily timeline is unclear in regard to the balance of academia and employment. All-in-all, Jack's

astounding work ethic and desire to better his life cannot be denied!] *Starting in 1936, he worked as a bartender for seven years at The State Recreation. For a short time, he was employed in air base construction at Pueblo, Colorado. His first salaries were 25 cents per hour and $15 per week.* [It is unclear which jobs paid these amounts.]

Eudora Wiese was born October 12, 1916, to Otto and Mina Oxtoby Wiese on a farm near Oakes, North Dakota, the eldest of five children. She graduated from Oakes High School (May 24, 1934). It had been decided early in her high school days that going to college was out of the question financially and that commercial subjects should be taken to prepare for office employment. In the fall of 1934, she started temporary work in the Dickey County Auditor's Office in Ellendale. In early 1935, she went to Bismarck where she worked as a secretary for a number of years at the North Dakota Workmen's Compensation Bureau and later as a secretary for the World War II Office of Price Administration. Her first month's salary was $65 which seemed like a fortune at that time. Room in a private home was $15 per month, and it took $15 to $20 for meals.

On June 6, 1943, Jack and Eudora were married at Trinity Lutheran Church in Bismarck.

Eudora and Jack on their wedding day, June 6, 1943

For three years, they farmed his father's place at Goodrich, ND. On September 28, 1946, they returned to Burleigh County, Menoken Township, Section 20, where they live today.

—Burleigh County: Prairie Trails to Hi-Ways, *page 397*

ONE TIME, I ASKED MOM, "If you knew that you were going to get married, why did you wait so long?" She stated matter-of-factly, "Because we had to work to save money to purchase a farm of our own."

After over six years of scrimping and saving before they married and during the first three years of marriage, Mom and Dad had banked enough cash to purchase a section (640 acres) in Burleigh County about ten miles east of Bismarck. Mom told me, "We moved onto the place on September 28, 1946, with $40 in the bank and a baby on the way!"

There was no harvest that fall from their very own soil and, therefore, no crop income. Our parents earned a steady income that carried them until harvest the next year by trading a case or two of eggs every week to a Bismarck mom-and-pop grocery store. It was the only grocery store that was open on a Sunday. After the heifers became "fresh" (gave birth), the cream/milk check from Schultz Creamery in Bismarck added to the weekly income.

The farmstead and acreage, purchased from Dad's uncle, Win Coman, consisted of a large, strongly built barn, a hog house, a cattle shed, and a very old house. Built in the nineteenth century, the house was a basic two-room structure with a one-room attic and a dirt-walled and -floored basement. It boasted an additional anteroom that served as foyer, shop, storage area, and catch-all space. Their "new" house was not much more than a one-and-a-half story shack! It lacked running water, an indoor bathroom, and electricity.

It was already inhabited by mice! Within my four-year collection of memories of that abode resides Mom's warning to "stay away from the mouse traps" that were placed around the room's perimeter on the cold, worn linoleum floor.

The dwelling had been vacant of humans for some time. According to neighbor Hilda Neugebauer's diary, the previous occupants, the Funstons, had moved to Sterling on April 7, 1946.

Jack and Eudora's firstborn, Jacqueline Joann, arrived at 12:59 p.m. on February 26, 1947, at St. Alexius Hospital in Bismarck, North Dakota. Dad remembered the farm thermometer registered a temperature of minus 2° F.

When Mom and Dad brought me home, their bedroom was just large enough for a double bed and a crib with about eighteen inches between the two; a cardboard wardrobe stood at the end of the bed. The room was approximately nine by ten feet. My crib was next to the window. Mom lined the crib with newspaper to prevent the wind from reaching me.

The almost-nonexistent barrier between the harsh North Dakota weather and the interior of the house consisted of the faded white stucco exterior, a horizontal lathe layer, absolutely no insulation, and the interior plaster wall—that was it! No wonder the wind blew in through the walls and around windows! Mom once said that, in the winter, the interior wall was covered with penetrating frost!

THE WINDSWEPT 640 ACRES that greeted Mom and Dad in 1946 were flat and treeless. Our parents soon changed the landscape. The Prairie States Forestry Project, simply called "The Shelterbelt," originated in the Dirty Thirties as President Franklin D. Roosevelt's response to years of drought and dust storms that resulted in significant soil erosion. Mom and Dad took advantage of the program by planting four groves with seedlings of a variety of trees totaling about four miles in length. These little fellows needed water if they were to mature into a green picture frame of the farmstead while slowing the incessant North Dakota wind, which eroded the rich topsoil.

Imagine this daily watering routine: Dad working all day in the field; Mom baking, cooking, cleaning, and washing and ironing clothes—all without electricity—gardening, and trying to keep up with me, a never-still toddler, while dusk turned to darkness. Together with a tired toddler, they drove a team of horses pulling a stone boat topped with two fifty-gallon barrels, plus three cream cans full of water, to the newly planted shelterbelts. Bucket by bucket, they laboriously watered these little stick-trees. Mom recalled that amid the sound of relentlessly swarming mosquitoes, my bedtime long overdue, I cried and splashed in the mud of the newly watered seedlings. For months, this daily watering schedule proved to be the key to the survival of these tenacious seedlings, despite the assault of wind, drought, hail, and grasshoppers.

Additionally, Dad and Mom were pioneers in another area of soil conservation—crop rotation. The method was new to our particular area of the prairie and immediately proved profitable! They took advantage of various educational opportunities to further their knowledge of new farming practices that would improve their land and the crops raised on those acres. They attended locally sponsored soil and water conservation programs and exhibits, gathering ideas they could put into practice in the hope of being financially rewarded.

The Bismarck Tribune – undated

Soil Conservation Farming Methods Pay for Pfeiffers

Adoption of soil conservation farming methods has brought about increased yields and a stabilization of income for Mr. and Mrs. Jack Pfeiffer, Menoken.

In 1945, when the farm they live on now was being farmed without any attention to a plan of soil conservation, the yield was low.

Now the Pfeiffers have a complete diversified plan in operation and with it things have picked up.

The Pfeiffers have a 3-year rotation—two years small grain and one year of corn or fallow. Their rotation includes a grass and a legume field with the cropping plan.

By shifting this field over the entire crop acreage, all of the land will get organic matter to build it up. It also adds to the needed hay-land for the livestock in the program.

That the program was stable was emphasized in 1949. Despite the fact that hail destroyed the grain crop, the Pfeiffers' income was higher than in 1948, when there was no hail.

The native pasture is supplemented by seeded grass on parts of the pasture. This provides early spring pasture, increasing the length of time the cattle can graze and thus cutting the costs of feeding.

Stubble mulch tillage on both summerfallow and on cropland has given good results too, Pfeiffer says. Yields of grain are about double the amount they were before this method of farming was started, Pfeiffer explains.

The new three-quarter mile field shelterbelt includes two rows of evergreens. Pfeiffer's plan included this at the beginning and it is already getting a good start.

STANDING IN AWE of real wild geese, part of the state Game and Fish department's outstanding exhibit in the small gymnasium of the World War Memorial building are 18-month-old Jacqueline Pfeiffer, daughter of Mr. and Mrs. J.C. Pfeiffer, Menoken and 9-month-old Richard Wagner, son of Mr. and Mrs. Elmer Wagner, 1516 Ave B. Not the stuffed variety, the birds are only part of the display of live North Dakota wildlife including deer, prairie dogs, raccoons and gophers. **The Bismarck Tribune, 1948**

ANOTHER BLESSING WAS bestowed upon our family on July 3, 1950. It's another girl! Janine Cheryl arrived at St. Alexius Hospital in Bismarck, North Dakota. Mom had urgently awakened Dad in the wee hours of the morning in order to get to the hospital before the newest addition to the family arrived. He responded that he couldn't immediately take Mom to the hospital. He had to milk the cows first! Despite this, they arrived at the hospital in time for a seven o'clock delivery.

Our old house and farm buildings had been electrified by the time of Janine's birth. We no longer lived and worked in the illumination of a small flame from kerosene lantern. Instead, with the flick of a switch, the sole light fixture lit the larger of the two rooms on the main floor.

Now then, imagine how excited Mom and Dad were when building our new house in 1951, knowing that the wonderful convenience of electricity would continue to provide light and energy to our new home! No longer did our abode depend on just one light bulb for illumination. Now every corner was filled with light. What a joy for Mom to have her daily work burdens eased with the assistance of electricity, running water, and an indoor bathroom in the new house! No more freezing on the way to the outhouse!

During the house-building process, Dad and I often went to the Anderson Lumber Yard in Bismarck to pick up building supplies. He seemed to be glad to

Janine in July 1951, during home building

have me with him. I'm sure Mom was pleased to be able to spend some time with just baby Janine. He'd take care of his business, and my four-year-old curiosity would prompt me to explore the bowels of the lumber barns.

As the house was being built during the summer, I recall reclining in the never-before-used bathtub, surrounded by Little Golden Books, feeling contentment as I gazed at the fluffy white clouds through the ceiling-less rafters.

We girls had our very own bedrooms. An added bonus was that my bedroom featured a walk-in closet. I remember feeling special when Mom thought to ask me what color I wanted my room to be painted. Without hesitation, I replied, "Blue." Blue is still my favorite color.

Our three-bedroom, one-bath home featured hardwood oak flooring, except in the bathroom, kitchen, and utility room where practical linoleum served. The living room sported a typical 1950s picture window and a front door showing three vertical rectangular-shaped windows. The lower part of the bathroom walls exhibited pink and gray tiles. I always thought that was an odd combination. In later years, I learned that those two colors were favored by former First Lady Mamie Eisenhower. When Janine and I were little, we thought it was a BIG house! No matter what the size, it was just right for our family!

The cost of the new house was $15,000—paid in cash! It completed a picture-perfect farmstead—white buildings topped with red asphalt shingles and white painted fences, all surrounded by lush, green shelterbelts.

The Menoken Community

OBSERVING THE INVISIBLE parameters of our Menoken community meant more than just having the same village name written on a stamped envelope. I saw the lifestyle of neighbor helping neighbor as the glue that held this rural society together.

Members of this cohesive group of local citizens held positions of public school and Sunday school teachers. I saw neighbors serving as 4-H leaders for community children. Families picnicked together, and after a sweaty day of work, they cleaned up and promenaded with each other at square dances. They raised funds for the local church when men hosted pancake suppers. Those jovial fellows could really flip pancakes!

Salty tears dropped as neighbors joyfully celebrated young adult marriages. Yet tears of sadness were noted as these same folks gathered at the Menoken Cemetery for the burial of dear friends.

I saw for miles as this bonded group of men helped each other with harvesting, sheep shearing, and working cattle. Community mothers graciously welcomed new folks to the area with tasty hotdishes and helpful hands.

As neighbor Zella Trauger once told the Pfeiffer sisters, "Nobody thought that they were better than the other one."

These activities and social gathering places were influential in shaping the characters of our authors during the 1950s.

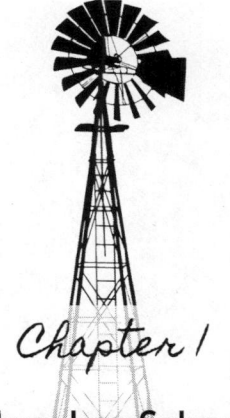

Chapter 1
Menoken School

SINCE KINDERGARTEN was not available at the time, my formal education began in the first grade in 1953 at the two-story stucco-sided Menoken Grade School.

Plenty of fresh air, sunshine, and light penetrated through the large windows of each room. The building boasted two classrooms (first through fourth grades—the primary room—and fifth through eighth grades—the upper-class room) on the top floor. There were also two small rooms (approximately nine by fourteen feet) on that floor: the library and, parallel to it, a quiet room with a single bed. It served as a calming environment for any student who might have a tummy ache and need to leave the classroom or who needed an undisturbed environment for making up a test.

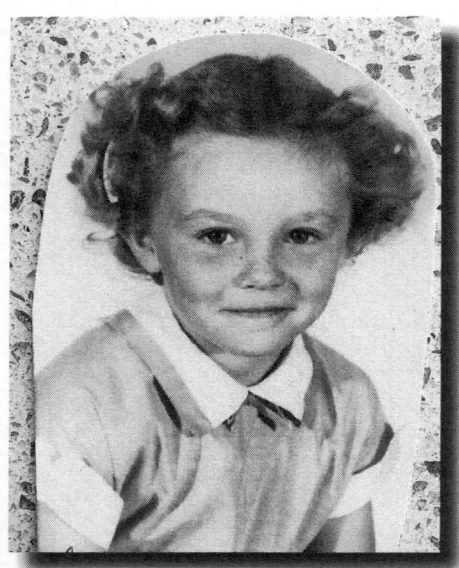
Jackie, first grade

The library included a mimeograph machine (forerunner of a copying machine) and a large, vintage paper cutter whose cutting arm reminded me of a French guillotine. Floor-to-ceiling wooden bookshelves housed dozens of hardback classics. Upon opening these books, the aroma of old paper wafted into my nostrils. As a fifth-grader, the red, royal blue, and bright gold spines of a book series led me to discover the writings of Louis L'Amour. His frontier stories captured my childhood interest. During my adult years, I learned that this author had been born and raised near Jamestown, North Dakota, less than 100 miles from our farm.

The building's lower level consisted of the furnace room, lunchroom, girls' and boys' restrooms, a storage room nestled underneath the wide stairway, and a teacher's apartment.

I was fortunate to have been a student of Mrs. Violette Arntz during my first four primary grades. Mrs. Arntz was a very tall, well-groomed, gifted lady who radiated a commanding presence! She loved her job, evidenced by her many smiles, and the students loved/liked and respected her! She was kind, firm, and fair.

Our Day

THE SCHOOL DAY BEGAN at nine o'clock with the Pledge of Allegiance. Students took turns for the honor of leading the Pledge while standing at the front of the entire room of students. All eyes were on the little flag that hung at a forty-five-degree angle near where the A-B-Cs began across the top of the blackboard the entire width of the room.

Following the recitation of the Pledge, lessons began with music class for all grades, first through eighth. This usually consisted of singing from several books, led by Mrs. Arntz's beautiful voice and flowing piano accompaniment. Sometimes we did round/circle dances such as "La Varsovienne," also called "Put Your Little Foot," which features a basic mazurka step. Anything that had to do with music and dancing was a favorite activity for Janine and me!

Besides music, Mrs. Arntz taught reading (including literature and poetry), penmanship, phonics, art, grammar, history, science, and geography. Only in hindsight have I realized how the exposure to places throughout the world from classroom books and from the *My Weekly Reader* magazine has influenced my adult life. The seed of my bucket list of places to visit in both the United States and the world was planted in a rural North Dakota classroom.

For instance, I yearned to visit the La Brea Tar Pits in urban Los Angeles, where animals had been swallowed by tar during the Ice Age; the patriotic Freedom Trail in Boston—just follow the red brick trail through the city; the subpolar capital of Iceland, Reykjavik, which uses geothermal energy for generating electricity and for heating; the nineteenth-century fairytale Neuschwanstein Castle in Bavaria, Germany; and so many more! Remember the book *Misty of Chincoteague* and the story of Pony Penning Day on Assateague Island, just off the coast of Virginia? Attending that event remains on my bucket list!

THE CLASSROOM SEATING arrangement never changed. First-grade students' desks were aligned in a row next to the east windows. I couldn't have been more excited to participate in the subject of coloring! I used the members of my new box of eight Crayola crayons with glee, selecting the appropriate color that was named within each circle on the page.

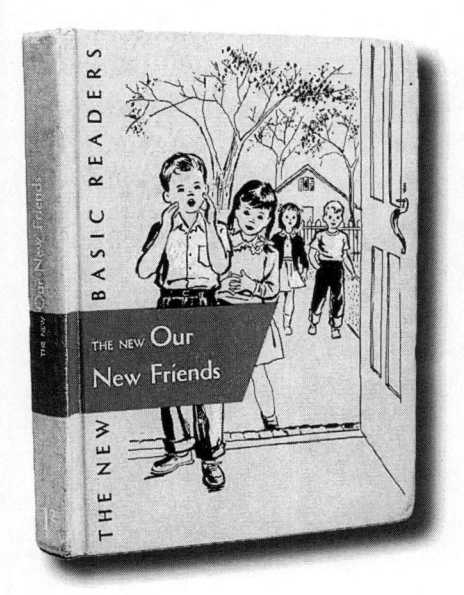

{ Janine }

New reading friends—Dick, Jane, Sally, Tim, Spot, Mother, and Father—were literary encouragers of repetitive word recognition. After all, in the 1950s, who didn't learn to read and increase reading capability with Dick and Jane?

Menoken School

MRS. ARNTZ HAD HER OWN classroom warning mechanism—the heel of her high-heeled pump. If students who were supposed to be quietly involved with their assignments were whispering as she was conducting a recitation class with a different grade level, five—count them, five—stomps with her heel on the polished hardwood floor served as her unspoken, "Quit whispering, and get back to work!"

This auditory warning system was also used to alert Mr. Arntz, our custodian. Mr. and Mrs. Arntz lived in the apartment beneath the primary classroom. The high-heel-stomp method served its purpose valiantly as our country school intercom.

When it was lunchtime, we students knew to be quiet for dismissal in order to be released row by row. Mrs.

Arntz said, "Turn [in our seats], stand, pass [walk]," and we moved in a courteous manner downstairs to the restrooms to wash our hands and then, orderly, proceeded into the lunchroom.

In a rural North Dakota school, where there was a fuzzy line (or maybe there was no line at all) between church and state, before eating our lunch, we always thanked the Lord for our food. We sang, "Noontime has come, the board is spread. Thanks be to Him, who gives us bread. Praise God for bread."

We agree that our school cook, Mrs. Lux, was the BEST! She treated us to all sorts of extra culinary pleasures not typically found in institutional cooking—treats such as homemade cookies, cakes, and caramel rolls. She was creative with the government-subsidized "mystery meat," rice, and beans. The meat had a delicious, well-browned flavor. Even though it was stringy in texture, it was very tasty. (We always wondered if it was horse meat, but we really didn't want to know.)

THE RICE WAS PRESENTED as Spanish rice, rice pudding, and some other kind of creamy rice main dish that did not agree with me. At one meal, Mrs. Arntz noticed I hadn't finished the creamy rice dish (this was not the first time I'd not eaten it), and she said I had to eat it before I could go out for the noon recess. I told her if I ate it, I'd get sick. She replied that I had to eat it anyway. I figured the only way I'd get outside to recess was to eat the stuff, vomit, and prove my point! That's exactly what happened! I never had to eat that rice dish again!

I also didn't care for the baked beans, not because of the taste but because of the sight. The shriveled white bean skins reminded me of maggots, and the beans looked like dog "urp." I almost gagged to look at the pile on my plate! I remember staring at the green wall of the lunchroom and concentrating on the taste (which wasn't bad), rather than the sight and texture!

Janine

MRS. LUX WAS A MIDDLE-AGED, aproned, black-hair-netted marvel in the school's kitchen. The first time I smothered a slice of her homemade white bread with peanut butter sweetened with honey, I thought I had died and gone to Heaven!

But it was her homemade sloppy joes, served on fresh-from-the-oven, lighter-than-air homemade buns, that completed the culinary masterpiece of school lunch menus for this student. Evidently, Dennis Trauger and Daryl Roberson thought so, too. Mrs. Lux served until the food ran out—no stopping after seconds. Dennis and Daryl always jumped into a sloppy joe competition each time that sandwich was served. Who would eat the most?

Usually, little-statured Daryl won the food race after consuming twelve sandwiches. His tummy must have been the size of a helium balloon. Both young gents were not embarrassed as they grossly expelled gas from both ends to obtain gastrointestinal comfort after the competition.

> *To settle her students after lunch recess, Mrs. Arntz read from a book for twenty minutes. Her enthusiasm while reading a story influenced our enjoyment of the written word.*

NO MATTER WHAT the weather, we always had a fifteen-minute recess in the morning and another in the afternoon. The playground equipment consisted of two sets of four swings, two teeter-totters, a merry-go-round, and a slide. I loved to swing! When soaring just a few feet above the ground into the air, I felt as if I were flying! Whee!

Students had been warned about being careful when exiting the swings from a high point in the swinging motion. Unfortunately, a high point for Dennis Trauger became a low point in his day as he flew through the air and landed on his arm, which resulted in the necessity of wearing a cast for a few weeks.

Tag was a popular outdoor game played during recess. The goal was to run from one base to the other base—the school's front steps to the flagpole—without being tagged by the person who was named "It." A young person nominated to be the catcher of runners, also known as "It," had a nearly impossible task of tagging/catching older, faster schoolmates."

A ball field lay adjacent to the playground equipment. It was used in the non-snowy season for playing softball and for running races. But in the wintertime, it became a perfect canvas for making a Fox and Geese game pattern.

Winter provided ingenious outdoor play opportunities! Keeping warm while battling frigid temperatures required several layers of clothing. Girls always wore dresses to school. It was the usual mode of dress for young ladies at the time. Corduroy pants were worn under my dress. Beneath those layers, brown cotton stockings (ugh!), held up by a contraption known as a suspendered garter belt, covered my legs. It wasn't fashionable, but it was practical! At least on Sunday, I was allowed to wear "dress-up" white cotton stockings.

The snow and cold wind on the prairie formed large snowbanks. With creative engineering—digging and scooping—the raw materials were transformed into a cozy snow cave. Large, rectangular snow blocks were hewed with the slice of a mittened hand and stacked to form an igloo or a barricade for the eventual snowball fight. Snow angels and snowmen often dotted the schoolyard.

The west side of the school property bordered the pasture of Mr. Ralph Mallard. A loose barbed wire fence was the only barrier between us students on school land and a most enticing, most exciting sledding hill! That fencing didn't stop us, however, and good ol' neighbor Mr. Mallard didn't seem to care. Sledding down that hill seemed to be a tradition at our school! All of the students participated in the joy of flying down the hill either on Radio Flyer wooden sleds with slick metal runners or on plastic flying saucer sleds. Be ready for that bump near the bottom! Recess was too short!

Recently, I realized that I had been given the opportunity to acquire the skill of memorization in my youth.

This awareness came to mind when I was in the presence of three other adults; only two of us were able to recall memorizing such pieces as The Preamble, The Gettysburg Address, *poems of American poets, and many songs of bygone days*—My Grandfather's Clock, Oh! Susanna, She'll Be Coming 'Round the Mountain, Marines' Hymn, *and hundreds more songs!*

When my own children were in public school, I learned that they had not been given the opportunity to develop the skill of memorization. Sadly, the worthy skill seems to no longer be important.

✕✕✕ *Jackie* ✕✕✕

Upon arrival each day, the American flag had been raised by Mr. Arntz to fly in the breeze from the tall silver flagpole. However, at the end of the school day, two students had the honor of practicing appropriate flag etiquette when lowering Old Glory.

I felt privileged when it was my turn to instruct a younger student in this act of patriotism. We showed respect for the flag by preventing it from touching the ground. As we reverently folded it into a tricorn shape representative of the cocked hats worn during the Revolutionary War, we took care that only stars on the field of blue showed on the top of the triangular shape of the folded flag. The aura surrounding us as we performed this ritual was one of the seeds of good citizenry taught in our country school.

Home Arts and Fine Arts

Janine

ONCE MRS. ARNTZ taught a home economics class just before Mother's Day. Each year homemade gifts would be showered on the mothers of her students in grades one through four. During one of my years in the primary grades, Gladys Goehring's recipe for Old-Fashioned Date Balls (page 255) would serve as the basis for a home economics lesson—a culmination of math, art, and science, along with the development of large and fine motor skills.

We students gathered in the lunchroom. Mrs. Arntz donned an apron and was at the helm. With cast-iron frying pans heating on the electric stove burners, Mrs. Arntz supervised the creation of this recipe. Butter was slowly melted and combined with other accurately measured ingredients. I did not like dates or the coconut that would be the treat's final coating. Mom did, though. Consequently, if it would bring happiness to her, I was excited to take part in the project!

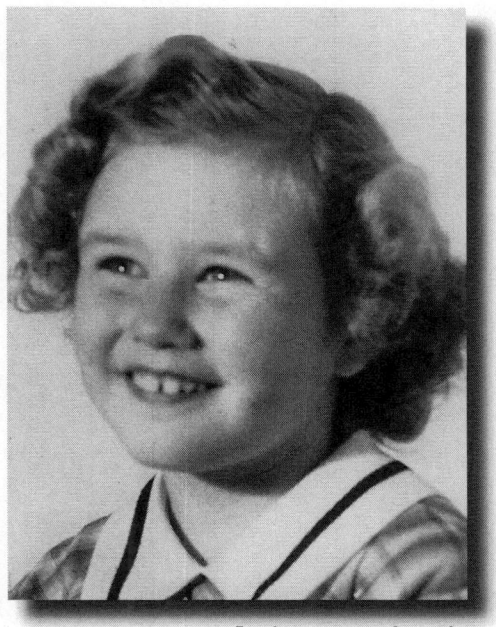

Janine, second grade

Each small amount of cookie mixture was quite hot in my little tender hands. Yet, I proudly shaped each spoonful of sweetness into a ball and rolled it into coconut. Four of these cookie balls fit appropriately within my homemade pink construction paper cone. I was not a very accomplished artist but did use my box of Crayola crayons to draw a stick version of Mom and me on the exterior paper surface. The entire gift was created from the heart of this little girl. Mom's joy upon receiving it kept me in "warm fuzzies" for a long time! Even while sharing this story, I have an abundance of happiness in its recollection.

I clung to this recipe for years as a part of my American prairie country school heritage. I brought the recipe out of storage and entered the cookies for judging in the highly competitive Iowa State Fair. They merited a beautiful second-place ribbon in the unbaked cookie class.

OUR FRIDAY AFTERNOON art class varied in content from week to week, but it usually followed the theme of the month. We would make decorations for the windows and one wall, craft gifts for parents for special occasions, or study art history. For instance, in February each student always made a Valentine card receptacle of one sort or another in art class. The finished products were then hung on the seven highly varnished wooden folding doors that separated the primary room from the upper grade room. My favorite receptacle was created by me in the third grade and was made out of printed wallpaper sprinkled with little pink flowers and pastel blue ribbon bows serenely resting on a pristinely white background in the shape of a twelve-inch heart. A six-inch piece of wallpaper, the same shape as the lower half of the heart, became the pocket that held valentines from classmates. The raw edges were securely stapled together. Carefully pleated white crepe paper simulating lace was neatly glued on top of the entire edge of the heart to cover the staples and finish the edge. It was beautiful!

Students usually made a Christmas gift for their parents. I still have the envelope holder that I made in the first grade. Four pieces of thin wood had been precut. The North Dakota state flower, the yellow-centered pink wild prairie rose, was outlined on the front panel of the thirsty wood and painted by each student. A week later, a coat of varnish completed the project.

MRS. ARNTZ WAS VERY artistic! Each month she drew an appropriate-to-the-month, freehand picture around the utilitarian calendar located on the right-hand side of the room-wide blackboard. Each colored chalk drawing was truly a work of art! In turn, each day a different student had the honor of crossing off the date on the calendar before the four o'clock dismissal time.

We studied arts in other ways, too. Mrs. Arntz served as the catalyst in exposing our young minds to the history of some of the Old Masters, who painted between 1600 and 1800. Rembrandt is a well-known example. One

Friday afternoon a month, she held a class known as Picture Study. Students were instructed to take out a clean sheet of paper from their desk. A three-inch-square picture with sawtooth edges and lickable gummed back (yuck!) was applied to the upper left-hand corner of the page. As Mrs. Arntz read a synopsis of the history of this classic artwork, the students were required to take notes and then write their own synopsis for eventual grading. By the time the year was over, each student had been exposed to some art history in elementary form.

Not only did this class introduce us to art as created by some of the Master Painters, but it also helped develop our brain capability to listen and record our thoughts about a subject. This is just one instance in which the teachers and school board in our little corner of rural America were united in preparing children for higher learning and a life beyond our rural community.

School Programs

EACH CHRISTMAS Mrs. Arntz directed an operetta. It gave all students, from grades one through eight, the opportunity to have a thespian experience whether they wanted it or not. Depending on the operetta, some students memorized speaking parts, all had group singing parts, and all were appropriately costumed. One of the most memorable operettas performed by our school was *The Little Blue Angel*. In fifth grade, Jackie played the part of a lonely princess who wondered if there was more to Christmas than receiving "just things." At the end of the program, it was revealed by the little blue angel—a classmate dressed in blue who stood behind and to the top of the evergreen Christmas tree—that there *was* something more important than "things." The best gift was the Christ Child. We sisters can still recall songs from that short opera.

Along with the traditional operetta, the entire school played in the rhythm band. The first-graders played the rhythm sticks. As the skill of rhythm matured, students graduated to playing the jingle tap, bells, triangles, hollow wood blocks, and sandpaper blocks. A seventh- or eighth-grader who was able to keep the rhythm of the music was awarded the honor of playing the one large drum. Jackie eventually worked up to the drum.

When we performed at the Christmas program, we were all decked out in festive red cotton capes with sparkling gold tinsel trim and red hats that resembled World War II garrison caps. We felt very special in our band uniforms! We usually marked time to about three Christmas songs. The capes had been made by a few mothers, including ours. Each year the capes emerged in a wrinkled state from the storage boxes but "magically" came to the students in a wrinkle-free condition.

Jackie

MY FIRST TIME on a stage occurred during a Christmas program even before I was old enough to attend school. It remains a pivotal point in my life! I don't know why this unprecedented event—a five-year-old performing in the school Christmas program—occurred, but Mrs. Arntz suggested I recite a four-line poem during the school Christmas program. I vividly remember this first time of being on any stage! I was so scared that I was shaking! The footlights (light bulbs screwed into a light bar) were hot on my face. My mind went blank! Mrs. Arntz prompted me, and I returned to reality and recited the poem. Then the most amazing thing happened! The audience clapped! A joyous feeling overtook me! I smiled and thought, "I like this! I want to do it again!" And thus, my intermittent but lifelong amateur stage career was launched!

After each year's program, the local school board, of which Dad had been a longtime member, gave every child, student, and family member a sweet treat. The children received brown paper lunch sacks of candy and whole peanuts; the adults received big red, crunchy, juicy Red Delicious apples wrapped in shiny paper. Oh, the aroma of the apples was divine!

When we were older, Janine and I helped Dad and

Mom and Howard Goehring put the candy in paper sacks—a sugar-high mixture of colorful ribbon candy, square pillow candy, sugar plums, and butter brickle, with salted peanuts in the shell thrown in for a more "healthful" treat! Over the years, Jake Schmidt, Kenny Trauger, and Howard Goehring played Santa. I think Dad played Santa one time. Janine remarked, "I remember being a little disappointed in the 'real Santa' because he hadn't shown up, and Dad had to substitute for him."

The Young Citizens League

THE MONTH OF APRIL brought a fun diversion from the classroom. The Burleigh County Young Citizens League (YCL) convention was a springtime highlight. The entire student body was treated to attending. The day's events occurred at the Bismarck Auditorium (now known as The Belle).

The purpose of YCL was to teach students about citizenship. After months of participating in our local school's YCL meetings at which parliamentary procedure was taught and respected, it was eye-opening and fun for us to join with students from other rural Burleigh

County schools to collectively show patriotism at work. Parents and teachers expected the adherence of good manners. After all, we were representing our Menoken School, community, and our families.

Students had the opportunity to be candidates for offices, engage in civics contests, and enter projects into a variety of competitions. One year, Jackie entered a know-your-state contest of some sort, with the result of her originally created two-by-three-foot plaster of Paris relief map of North Dakota winning a prize ribbon.

Janine ONE OF MY FONDEST fifth-grade memories of this convention was having served as Robert Clarys's campaign manager for the office of county vice president. Robert was two years my senior and definitely an introvert. I had my work cut out for me when creating a persuasive campaign speech. It can be difficult to showcase a somber, quiet young man as the person for this public job! However, he won the election for this seat and proved to be an accomplished man for the position!

During the school year, we students learned the *Y.C.L. Song* as part of the protocol of our monthly school meeting. Because of the singing practice at school, we would be able to participate in a rousing, marching rendition sung at the convention.

Y. C. L. Song
Words and Music by Arthur E. Thompson, former State Superintendent of Public Instruction, North Dakota.
Introduction
1. The Y. C. L. was founded to preserve our land, Make school more grand, By home to stand; With courage and with loyalty give heart and hand, Ev'ry day make dreams come true. . . . . .
2. Good citizens are we each day we strive along, With work and song A happy throng, We work for the community where we belong, Thinking well of ev-'ry-one. . . . . .
CHORUS
The Y. C. L. for school The Y. C. L. for land, We pledge with these for home, These three with heart and hand.

Jackie

WHEN THE CONVENTION paused for the noon meal, students walked a few blocks to the Patterson Hotel for the traditional meal of chicken à la king. There must have been a practical reason for that dish to be repeated year after year. Perhaps it was easy to make for a crowd and not very expensive. In my estimation, it wasn't worth repeating!

Janine

I DIDN'T MIND eating this blah-looking food for dinner, chicken à la king. But then, I've never been too picky about food. More than likely, most rural meat-and-potatoes-eating children had never seen the likes of such food. I surmise that either much food was scraped into the garbage or the parental "eat what is put in front of you" lesson was echoing within the minds of youngsters. I always ate what was put in front of me. Still do!

Several parents formed a carpool that took the students the ten miles to Bismarck. But the highlight of the day was the return mode of transportation—riding the Northern Pacific Railway from Bismarck to Burleigh, which was the original name given to the NP's stop at Menoken. The Burleigh train depot was situated on the south side of the tracks from the Menoken Post Office, across old U.S. Highway 10.

The eastbound passenger train departed each afternoon after four o'clock. To keep us occupied prior to gathering at the depot, intervening minutes were spent perusing the aisles of Woolworth's located across the street from the Bismarck depot. I recall the time when, as nine- and six-year-olds, Jackie and I had left home in the morning with Mom having given each of us a treasured paper dollar. There was an entire store of inventory within Woolworth's to capture our dollar bills. But since our family was a steady customer of that five-and-dime, I already knew what I would receive in trade for some of that dollar. I left the store proud as punch with an unsharpened red marking pencil—just like Mrs. Arntz used to grade papers!

Burleigh County Play Day

ONE OF MY FAVORITE times during the school year was the Burleigh County Play Day, which occurred the last week of the school year in May. Arithmetic testing and spelling bees were held in the morning, but the fun happened in the afternoon. Other country school students from Driscoll, Moffit, Sterling, and McKenzie came to Menoken for running

Jackie

races, the gunny sack race, the three-legged race, the potato race, high jump, broad jump, and a softball game. The Hall was the venue for the awards ceremony, where winners collected their coveted little colored ribbons. The races, high jump, and broad jump were my strengths. My treasured ribbon collection lived in a shoebox on my closet shelf.

Eighth-Grade Graduation

Janine

DENICE TRAUGER, Terry Oster, Dennis Clarys, and I were classmates the entire eight years in Menoken, with Judy and Janice McCormick and Rodney Medearis having joined our class in later years. The finale of our eight years of elementary school transpired at the celebrated Burleigh County Eighth-Grade Graduation Exercises at Bismarck Junior College (now Bismarck State College). Young adolescents from all of the county's rural schools were honored and presented with diplomas. From that day forward, my classroom environment completely metamorphosed into big-city school.

I was a frightened ninth-grader at Simle Junior High, Bismarck, and later at Bismarck High School with the completion of my secondary education. Jackie and I have concurred that, as country kids, we always felt beneath the lifestyle of our new city classmates. For me, this defeatist emotion served as a weapon against my self-esteem, continually playing over and over as a broken record titled "You'll never be able to achieve above and beyond what the city kids had." It was crushing! Thankfully, this proved to be false. I eventually overcame this counterfeit belief of rejection and soared with a newfound freedom to learn and adapt in all of my classes and activities.

Chapter 2
Community Challenges and Progress

PEOPLE LIVING on the prairie in the 1950s faced multiple seen and unseen threats. North Dakotans such as the Pfeiffers rose to overcome those challenges by facing them head-on, thereby welcoming advances in medicine, technology, and inventive sciences. Through their windows, I noticed small bottles of iodine and Mercurochrome holding residence inside mirror-fronted bathroom home medicine chests. With a drop of either of those red liquids and topped with a flesh-colored Band-Aid, cuts and scrapes of the skin healed quickly.

However, it was those sneaky unseen threats of a higher order in the forms of disabling and life-threatening viruses and bacteria along with government world greed that were the nemeses of life. Scary? Indeed!

Observing over and beyond our Menoken community,

I witnessed the fact that no one was naturally immune to these possible life-threatening perils. I shudder to think of the potential path of destruction to human life we might've walked had not brilliantly gifted scientists and government leaders opened a progressive pathway for a better life on the prairie. In my opinion, though, the game changer for rural progress—electricity!

Rural Electrification

THE VISTA OF OUR CORNER of rural America was completely uplifted when rural electrification came to Menoken Township in 1949, a full thirteen years after the Rural Electrification Act of 1936 provided federal loans to newly formed cooperative electric power companies for the installation of distribution systems in isolated, rural areas. Rural electrification was a breath of fresh air to those living in rural America.

The electric power lines of the Rural Electrification Administration (REA) ran parallel to our land. Neighbor Marlys Neugebauer Frandsen provided excerpts

From the Diary of Hilda Neugebauer

Aug. 24, 1948: Two guys from the Boyer Electric Company put up the meter box on the pole in our yard.

Sept. 8, 1948: Two guys from the REA put up the 3 wires from the meter box pole to the next one.

Sept. 10, 1948: A man from Koenig Electric, Mandan, stopped in to see about wiring our house for the REA.

Sept. 14, 1948: Three men from the Koenig Electric in Mandan came to wire our house this p.m.

Sept. 15, 1948: The Koenig Electric finished wiring our house at noon. Cost: $199.34. Have lights in all 3 rooms, 2 wall switches and 3 outlets. Have fluorescent light in the kitchen, wall switch for front room and pull switch for bedroom.

Sept. 17, 1948: We bought an electric automatic iron (General Electric) from Koenig Electric and also the light fixtures. That's included in the $199.34 for wiring our house.

Sept. 20, 1948: The REA guys came this a.m. and put up the meter so got electric lights. Sure nice and light in our house to read and write, etc.

Sept. 27, 1948: We've used 3 kilowatts of electricity since last Monday. Can use 40 a month for $5.00.

Oct. 20, 1948: Today is the first month we pay the electric light bill. Was $5.00. Used only 18 kilowatts this last month.

from the diary of her mother, Hilda, that documented the progress of electrification on the Neugebauers' farm.

Marlys shared with us, "I remember the poles being put in on...what we called 'Pfeiffers' Hill.' I could hardly wait for the day when I could turn on the switch and have light."

Unseen Threats

IN 1954, THE LOCAL SCHOOL was often the community's venue for the mass inoculation of all U.S. school children when the Dr. Jonas Salk polio vaccine was administered for protection from the deadly virus. United States school children also received the smallpox inoculation at school. That vaccine was administered in the 1950s, even though it had been introduced into society by Edward Jenner in 1798.

We sisters received our childhood inoculations for smallpox, whooping cough, diphtheria, measles, mumps, rubella, and polio on the designated day when our county school nurse, Miss Jean Norton, came to Menoken School. The vaccinations required when we were babies had been given by our pediatrician at Quain and Ramstad Clinic in Bismarck.

With the clean smell of antiseptic permeating the air in our school lunchroom, a makeshift clinic was laid out on an eight-foot table. As a line formed by our schoolmates approached the nurse, she used a white cotton ball dabbed with alcohol to clean an area over the muscle above our elbow before giving the injection. Depending on the inscribed entries on our updated vaccination record, we received one or more needle pricks with life-saving vaccine.

In 1962, the (Albert) Sabin version of polio vaccine was introduced, using a weakened form of the live virus. The pink serum was "hidden" in a snow-white sugar cube. Our palates noted an enticing sweet flavor when the cube was placed upon the tongue. Quickly, though, this flavor turned surprisingly bitter!

We cannot recall the polio disease having afflicted our neighbors and friends in the Menoken community. However, neighbor Hilda Neugebauer recorded in her personal diary, "Aug. 15, 1946, polio epidemic is bad in ND, MN is worst."

ANOTHER UNSEEN THREAT was from the skies in the form of Soviet nuclear warheads. During our elementary school years, the U.S. was engaged in the Cold War with the USSR. That knowledge was a little frightening! All school children had air raid drills that consisted of leaving the chairs that were attached to our desks and folding our bodies underneath the desks (a lot of good that would have done!).

Mrs. Arntz took that safety precaution farther; if the school was notified that the Soviet planes had targeted the small village of Menoken for a nuclear attack (not likely), the students were to walk in an orderly fashion down the stairs to the furnace room, which would serve as our fallout shelter. The KFYR radio station located about two miles north of the school (and one-quarter mile north our house) was the closest official fallout shelter. The sod-covered, igloo-looking structure erected alongside the small, square, white stucco radio station building would not have been able to hold many people! The rest would have been toast!

CHALLENGES AND SOLUTIONS on the prairie led to progress for mankind:
- Fine-point needles through which life-saving serums were injected.
- America withstanding world leaders' threats of nuclear destruction.
- Darkness broken into immediate light with a single flick of a switch.

Connecting to the Outside World

ONE COULD HAVE FELT so alone while pursuing a living on the vast prairie! Stressful, never-ending wind could actually drive one literally mad! Farm homes located distantly apart delayed communication from neighbor to neighbor. Continual, laborious drudgery fueled by the need to better oneself was life's certain singular motive. Lack of progressive telecommunications connecting folks to the outside world brought isolation.

Just as sure as my whirligig twirled, so, too, came communication advances in our area. The camaraderie of the Menoken residents was a partial stopgap to feelings of solitude. Yet the convergence of various forms of communication marvels, together with the Pfeiffers' desire to reach beyond the confines of their farm and community, served as the invitation for new forms of communication to enter their lives.

Janine

DURING THE 1950s, our radio was a constant companion in our kitchen. The day always began with a turn of the knob to radio station KFYR 550 AM, Bismarck. The radio was our lifeline for updated livestock and grain markets, news, weather, and music. Mom listened intently to Martha Bohlsen's radio homemaking program as new recipes and homemaking tips were shared by this professional home economist. A radio homemaker was more than a homemaking teacher to her listeners. Her voice became the welcoming sound of friendship and camaraderie.

We were one of the last families in our community to purchase a television; our first appeared in 1956! The TV was a massive piece of furniture—a blond-colored cabinet surrounding a small television screen. With the first click of the dial, the picture did not appear! Was it broken already? After the picture tubes had a brief warm-up session, we watched Kit Carson

> *Although the nearest library was about twelve miles away in Bismarck, we could not have a library card because we didn't have a Bismarck address. Despite that misfortune, Janine and I are both avid readers. We suspect that is due in part to our parents planting the "reading seed." Our home was filled with a diverse group of magazines and newspapers that kept Mom and Dad informed.*
>
> ✕✕✕ *Jackie* ✕✕✕

ride his horse, Apache, across the screen into the dusty sunset. However, we had to imagine the colors of the sunset because the picture was in black and white only! We learned that the scene became even more visible by adjusting the rabbit ears (antennae) located on top of the TV. Aluminum foil came to our rescue to achieve a clearer picture. Becoming novice electrical engineers, we wrapped pieces of foil around the tip of each antenna. Voilà—clearer picture!

OCTOBER 19, 1959—a great day! Our farm home was equipped with the most modern form of personal communication at this time—a telephone! At the time we began subscribing to BEK Telephone Company's service, Dad and Mom felt that a telephone would give us instantaneous chatting capabilities with Grandpa and Grandma Pfeiffer in Bismarck and Grandma Wiese in Oakes.

However, we didn't always have instant use of this exciting new portal to the broader world. We were on a party—not private—line. Therefore, if another family on our line was talking on their phone to a caller, we had to patiently wait our turn in order to make our outgoing call. Likewise, if someone were trying to call our home, they would continually get a "beep, beep, beep" until the party-line member had discontinued the conversation.

The black, rotary-dial phone mounted on the north kitchen wall did indeed launch our family into the rapidly improving world of telephone communication!

I LISTENED AS VOICES of radio personalities were welcomed as guests into the Pfeiffers' home. The first *hello* that Eudora spoke into the telephone receiver was uttered with a smile on her face. But to hear Jackie and Janine squeal with delight when ol' Apache kicked up dirt on the television screen's picture—now that was pure pleasure!

Chapter 3
The Churches

Jackie

THERE WERE TWO CHURCHES in or near the village of Menoken, St. Hildegard Catholic Church and the Menoken Methodist Church. My Christian foundation was influenced by my family's involvement in the Methodist church. In 1949, a group of community members, including our parents, purchased a Presbyterian church built in 1903 from Stewartsdale, an abandoned settlement southwest of Menoken. The building was moved to an empty lot in Menoken, establishing the home of the Menoken Methodist Church congregation.

Everyone who was involved in church activities and was not Roman Catholic, participated at the Methodist Church. A traveling minister, the Reverend Edward Parker, presided on Sundays. Our neighbor to the north,

"Grandma" Mabel Salter, faithfully took Janine and me, and her granddaughters Patty and Janny to Sunday school.

I left the house with a coin-filled hankie that contained my offering for "those poor children in Africa," as relayed by my Sunday School teacher, Mrs. Salter. Mom made sure that the coins were secure in my little makeshift purse, so much so that sometimes Mrs. Salter needed to loosen the knot in order for me to place my offering into the felt-bottomed brass collection plate.

Menoken Methodist Church

I never questioned what happened to the offering after it left my little hankie coin holder. I just had faith that I was helping some unknown less-fortunate child. ("It is more blessed to give than to receive," Acts 20:35, teaches that there is joy in the act of giving when it is done with pure motives.) Our parents subtly taught this lesson by their acts of kindness.

Everyone called Mrs. Salter "Grandma." She and my Grandma Pfeiffer showed me what unconditional love was all about!

Mrs. Jenny Dance, the local postmistress, was the Sunday school superintendent. I received my first Bible from her on January 24, 1954, as a "good attendance" gift. It was a King James Version, probably the only version widely published at that time, and it contained many words that were too advanced for a third-grader.

There was a period of time when Mrs. Dance presided over the Good News Club. After school was dismissed at four o'clock on Tuesdays, a small contingency of grade-school students hiked a quarter mile to Mrs. Dance's white house with green trim, which was located across the road from the Methodist Church. Entering through the white picket gate revealed an expansive lawn bordered by large trees. When I passed through, it felt as if I were entering into a secret world protected by the perimeter of tall bushes and trees. The path led to the back door of her big house, which opened into a little utility area housing a white chest-type freezer that contained after-school treats. We students continued through the kitchen and into the living room where we practiced our "how to be a proper guest" manners and had a little midweek Sunday school lesson. Our youthful voices sang the official Good News Club song before each lesson. This song was etched within our minds decades ago. If you know it, sing along with us.

> *Good news, good news, Christ died for me.*
> *Good news, good news, now I believe.*
> *Good news, good news, I'm saved eternally.*
> *That's wonderful extra good news. Amen.*

The seed of faith, which is needed to be open to God's grace, had been planted at my baptism at Trinity Lutheran Church in Bismarck on August 3, 1947, but it was watered and fertilized at the Methodist Church in Menoken. I liked attending Sunday school. It featured music, a flannel graph story, and a project of some kind that supported the Bible lesson of the day.

We learned so many songs that were built on Bible stories. While attending an ecumenical Bible study as an adult, I realized that other Protestant faiths taught the same songs that I had learned at the Menoken Sunday School. The songs of my youth support my adult faith today.

Janine

SPEAKING OF SONGS, occasionally Mom and Dad would sing duets in church. Their beautiful voices blended so well together. From the oak twirling-seat piano stool, Carmen Owen accompanied Dad and Mom. *The Old Rugged Cross* and *In the Garden* were favorites. As a little girl, I would sit next to Jackie on the hard, wooden pew and listen with pride as my daddy and momma shared their gifts of music. None of our other neighbors and friends with whom we worshiped in the community shared their musical gifts as Mom and Dad had.

IN THE SUMMER, the church youth enjoyed a week of Vacation Bible School. It's strange now to think that one of the reasons we looked forward to Bible school was so that we could eat bologna sandwiches! It was the only time we were treated to bologna sandwiches. Since our farm provided an abundance of home-grown beef, pork, and poultry, purchasing processed meat was a rarity. The added bonus of the treat was that the bologna was placed between buttered slices of Mom's homemade bread. The sandwiches were wrapped in wax paper and then packed into a black metal lunch box. Outdoor recess included games such as The Farmer in the Dell, Red Rover, and other circle games. Snack time followed with donated-by-moms cookies and mouth-staining Kool-Aid.

Jackie

WHEN I BECAME of confirmation age as an eighth-grader, our family returned to its German Lutheran roots, and we faithfully attended Trinity Lutheran Church in Bismarck. Our parents were married at that church, and I was baptized there at five months of age. Our family usually sat in the front row of the balcony. It gave me a warm feeling to look down upon the congregation to see Grandpa and Grandma Pfeiffer seated in their traditional location. I liked the way the service began; the four-part *a capella* choir would sing, "The Lord is in His holy temple. Keep silent, keep silent, before Him. Keep silent, keep silent, before Him. Amen." I loved singing to the musical strains produced by the big pipe organ, which was expertly played by Mr. Clarion Larsen. It was exhilarating!

I enjoyed attending the confirmation class on Saturday mornings during my eighth and ninth grades. Pastor Nicolai (Pastor Nic, as he was fondly called) and Pastor Lutness shared the teaching. Discussion was encouraged, and memorization from *Luther's Catechism* was mandatory. The class of sixty-seven students was confirmed in May 1961.

Previously, I mentioned our German Lutheran roots. When visiting with Mom's sister, Aunt Merna Treeby, at her family's ranch near Hecla, South Dakota, I was pleased to learn how being a Lutheran had been passed from generation to generation. Merna shared a heartwarming story of how my great-grandmother, Martha, gathered her grandchildren around her kitchen table on Sunday afternoons and taught them from *Luther's Catechism* in the German language.

WE ARE PLEASED to share an update on our family's original church home. Since its construction in 1903, the church building metamorphosed multiple times from one denomination to the next holding worship services inside its walls. In 2017, it became The Menoken Crossroads Cowboy Church. Menoken resident Patty Salter Ennen relayed to us that Beard's Arena, about six miles south of Menoken, had been the previous location of the area's cowboy church. However, upon learning of the availability of the town's church building, purchase of the site was made for one dollar. New life was given to the community's spiritual home in the center of town when thousands of dollars of donations backed a complete building renovation, including the addition of running water, an indoor bathroom, new windows, drapes, and carpet, along with fresh paint for the interior and exterior, a new roof, and removal of the rotted church steeple. Hanging on an interior wall of the newly refurbished church is a memorial collection of stories and pictures that lovingly honor the founding influencers of the Menoken Methodist Church, Mrs. Jenny Dance and Mrs. Mabel Salter, whose heartbeats were the very lifeblood and soul of the church.

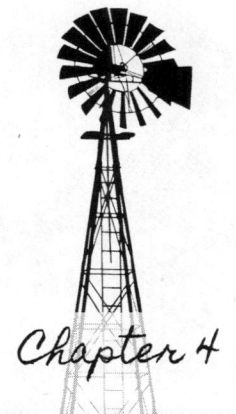

Chapter 4
Menoken at Play

EVERY COMMUNITY NEEDS a place to gather. Menoken Town Hall (always called "the Hall" in our community) had been built at the east end of town in 1914 at a cost of $4,700. Dad was the perpetually elected secretary of the Menoken Township Board. As a board member, the operation of the Hall was his responsibility. He made sure the building was prepped and primed for events.

Beneath the beautiful hardwood floor lay the bowels of the building, complete with a dank, musty odor and a coal-fired furnace. No running water! Two-hole wooden outhouse service only! Whether used for reading or other necessary maneuvers for good health, some fine citizen kept a supply of toilet paper and Montgomery Ward catalogs behind its doors. Thank goodness!

Main Street, Menoken, with the Hall at the right

Those amenities—or lack of—did not deter community members from gathering within the Hall's generous interior space for county and national political elections, square dances, local 4-H meetings and achievement shows, anniversary celebrations, bridal and baby showers, community theatre productions, Burleigh County rural schools spring Play Day awards ceremonies, baton twirling lessons, and Menoken Homemakers Club events. As of this writing, the Hall is no longer in use.

Janine IN OUR GROWING-UP YEARS, community square dances in the Hall began at eight in the evening on the last Saturday in September and continued monthly through May. Ray Schaeffer traveled from Bismarck to spin the records and call the square dance moves. Women and girls took this opportunity to dress the part of a fashionable square-dancing partner. A net crinoline slip and lace-ruffled pettipants flirtatiously peeked from beneath the full circular square-dance skirt when the wearer was twirled by her partner. Decorative metallic rick-rack applied to our costumes shimmered as we do-si-doed to Mr. Schaeffer's call. Dennis Trauger and I were usually partners. We joined with three other couples in our square as Mr. Schaeffer's calling moved us through myriad formations and positions.

Aside from square dancing, my favorite dances were those with Mom as my partner. She twirled me around

The cast of *Leave It to Grandma,* performed by Menokenites at the Hall in March 1953. From left: (front) Delvin Owen, Eudora Pfeiffer (playing Grandma), Ellen Sherman, and Howard Goehring; (back) Clarice Wachal, Jack Pfeiffer, Ruth Funston, Leon Owen, Alice Miller, Ruth Small, and Kenny Trauger

the dance floor during a waltz or two-step or even a bouncy polka. I felt lighter than air as I soared with happiness and love for my momma! Even as an adult, I shut my eyes and recall the buoyancy of those moments.

At ten o'clock, the women laid out the vast board of homemade sandwiches and cakes brought for lunch. Maureen Dance Kershaw was the BEST cake baker in the community! As I stood in the lunch line, my eyes perused the lineup searching for Maureen's Devil's Food Cake (page 256) covered with chocolate frosting and chopped English walnuts. To this day, Maureen credits neighbor Peggy Owen for this recipe.

Jackie

DURING THE SQUARE dance, when the clock ticked past my bedtime in my younger years, I often burrowed into the pile of woolen winter coats that had been casually layered upon a large, wooden table in a corner of the stage. After having found Mom's dusty pink wool coat with gray faux fur collar, I fell asleep wrapped within its folds. I felt surrounded by love!

Sweeping compound, with its distinct odor, and wide bristle brooms appeared from the closet after the dance was over at midnight. Oiled sawdust compound was sprinkled onto the hardwood floor as a dust collector. The floor was meticulously swept clean in courtesy to the next group using the building. Our family was usually the last to leave, as Dad had the key and made certain the fire in the furnace was out and the door was locked. Mom often said, "We don't leave until the last dog is hung."

ANOTHER COMMUNITY gathering spot was the Menoken Grove, commonly known as "the picnic grounds." As the crow flies, it was one mile east of our house across Jake Salter's field. Most of the surrounding farm ground was relatively flat. Yet, from our house, we could only see the treetops of the outdoor community gathering center that lay in the peaceful Apple Creek valley. Nature had provided mature, shady trees for picnicking comfort. A well-used dusty gravel road ran perpendicular to the Grove's entrance.

Our family enjoyed the refreshing coolness of the trees several times each summer: the end-of-school-year picnic, the Burleigh County 4-H picnic, the church picnic, the Bismarck Elks picnic, and the Homemakers Club picnic come to mind.

Mom always brought a large Tupperware container of potato salad. Hers was the *very best* tasting, and many people knew it. Consequently, there was never any left to take home. However, we had an abundance of eggs and potatoes, and Mom often made potato salad just for our family. Because we had so many eggs, she'd often make an angel food cake, which took one dozen egg whites; then she'd use the yolks to make egg noodles. We ate organically even before that practice was popular.

Depending on which organization sponsored the picnic, a variety of activities was available—softball, Tug-of-War, foot races, or pony rides.

When Mr. Sam Trauger, father of our neighbor Kenny Trauger and commonly known to us as Grandpa Trauger, drove onto the picnic grounds with his Ford pickup pulling a horse trailer loaded with Shetland ponies, we sisters were excited to divorce ourselves from our present activities and ride the gentle ponies. Similar to the repetition of a carnival ride, this was just another "walk in the park" for the group of equine members of this pony-riding business. Don't ask us why, but Trixie, the little black-and-white Paint pony, was our favorite! Every year, we each climbed into the black leather saddle cinched around Trixie's middle, placed our tennis-shoed feet into the stirrups, and awaited Grandpa Trauger's riding directions. We already knew horseback-riding protocol. It was one of our daily childhood modes of recreation. Therefore, when we each sat atop Trixie, we felt as though we were experienced horsewomen riding among a group of inexperienced city kids.

Sweet satisfaction during these hot North Dakota afternoons came from an ice cream truck offering vanilla, strawberry, chocolate, and maple nut (our favorite) cones, and from the generous slices of juicy, red watermelon cut and served by fathers in the group.

At a gathering of some of our former neighbors on July 4, 2016, Judy Goehring Miller shared with us that a plaque which honored Dad's volunteer efforts with the Burleigh County 4-H program is to this day displayed at Menoken Grove.

In 2016, former Menoken neighbors gathered on the Fourth of July to reminisce. From left, Marlys Neugebauer Frandsen, Janine Pfeiffer Knop, Linda Ehlers Schwengler, Judy Goehring Miller, JoAnn Goehring Schrenk, Jackie Pfeiffer McGregor, Marge Lein Perkins, Maureen Dance Kershaw

Chapter 5
Clubs

HARNESSING THE PRAIRIE demanded a focused family lifestyle. An unspoken chant—Arise early. Retire late—was the impetus that cradled the vitality of a workday's "bread and butter" cadence.

I noted that family unity was life's chapter title, with community cohesiveness as the subchapter. Group organizations provided a bonding of inhabitants living within the dusty borders of history's surveyed township lines.

Active 4-H and Homemakers clubs served that purpose in the Menoken community. Not only did membership allow personal growth, but it also captured the fragrance of personalities and talents of friends and neighbors.

This was the rhythm of the prairie.

JACKIE AND JANINE matured into learned young women in the nine-year season they were each members of the two Menoken 4-H clubs. Why, you wouldn't believe how the lessons of 4-H projects opened their minds to the learning of new skills. Aromas of freshly baked blueberry muffins and mouthwatering cherry pies drifted through open kitchen windows into the farmyard where I stood. I would catch a glimpse of a newly sewn, carefully pressed garment attentively placed on a hanger and poised for judging at the 4-H dress review in Bismarck. Jackie's instinctive love of horses and Janine's innate love of cattle were the catalysts in becoming accomplished 4-H livestock handlers. Mind you, though, the skills they learned through 4-H were all due to the patient teaching and encouragement of Eudora and Jack.

4-H WAS A VERY LARGE part of our lives. The youth organization was instrumental in shaping our ability and confidence in the skills that we developed. It allowed us to be "big fish in a little pond." By the time we reached the "big pond," college and beyond, we had acquired some experience in leadership, communication abilities, organizational adeptness, presence of mind, and a myriad of life skills. 4-H membership presented a host of projects appealing to a range of interests, which culminated in training a young person for much more than homemaking and farming practices.

I WAS ABLE TO JOIN two 4-H clubs at age ten. One was the girls' club, the Menoken Busy Workers 4-H Club (established in 1929 as Cheerful Stitchers). Girls could enroll in agricultural projects in the boys' club. That appealed to me, so I joined the Menoken Progressive (established in 1932). Dad and Howard Goehring were the group's leaders.

Jackie

MY FIRST GIRLS' CLUB project was to make items I would use while sewing—a wool-stuffed wrist pincushion (the lanolin in the wool prevents pins and needles from rusting), a needle storage case, and a scissors case. Mom was one of the original recyclers! The needle and scissors cases were cut from a good quality, brown, felted wool hat she had worn when she was a single career woman. (I thought it was a shame to cut up that hat.)

With threaded sharp needle, my hand-sewing skills produced a rectangular floral print dresser scarf. I wanted it to be perfect, so I used the hem gauge to measure the distance for *each* and *every* stitch! By using this measuring method, I trained my eyes to quantify short distances without the aid of a measuring tool. Additionally, this skill has continued to benefit me even outside the sewing realm. I am able to look at a section of wall and determine the exact spot where a picture needs to be hung in order to achieve a pleasing visual symmetry. No yardstick or plumb line necessary!

Using Mom's treadle sewing machine, the first garment I constructed was a gathered skirt made from floral print feed sack fabric. It was cheery with vivid yellow flowers and grass-green leaves printed on a white background. I could hardly wait to make it and start wearing it! In the mid-twentieth century, flour and animal feed could be purchased in fifty-pound or more fabric sacks. The bonus was a piece of fabric measuring approximately thirty-six inches wide by forty-three to fifty inches long.

The gathered skirt project taught several basic sewing techniques—regulating the speed of a treadle sewing machine, straight stitching, gathering, inserting a zipper, and hand hemming. The skirt received a blue ribbon, the first of many to come within the nine years that I exhibited in the clothing project. At the beginning, sewing was sometimes frustrating, but it was also very rewarding.

When I became a teenager, Dad told me, "You can have all the clothes you want, but you have to make them." I wonder if he ever regretted saying that, because I took full advantage of purchasing fabric with his blank checks! During the summer, I took the opportunity to constantly sew. Creating both the required garments for exhibit at local and county achievement days and garments just for fun occupied my summer days. As my sewing ability improved, awards came my way in both 4-H clothing construction contests and the North Dakota Make It Yourself with Wool contests.

The 4-H clothing project opened the door for creative thinking with fabric and thread. However, it was Mom's assistance, encouragement, and attention to detail that instilled great gratification within me at the completion of each sewing project. She often gave me this phrase of wisdom: "Think, Jackie, think!" These words were not only appropriate at that time but also carried over to other situations in my young life. Even today, I often recall those words and take them to heart!

My 4-H sewing project was the impetus of a future adulthood hobby. I have constructed such items as undergarments, dresses, tailored suits and coats, various crafts and quilts, and a variety of unique community theatre costumes. But the most creatively challenging undertaking—and the most fun—was designing

Victorian-era millinery fashions for the entire female cast in the Ascot scene of the production of *My Fair Lady!*

Besides sewing, there was a plethora of 4-H projects that I tackled, enabling me to become a more skilled, well-rounded individual. Each project required record keeping. Therefore, my summer calendar was completely filled with preparing items for exhibit as well as completing all of the necessary paperwork.

Janine

SEWING THROUGH 4-H also fostered memorable growth for me. Mom was an impeccable seamstress exemplifying the art of needle and thread excellence. Her nonverbal expectation was that if Jackie and I gave our best effort to learning the art of sewing through the adage "practice makes better," we young seamstresses would soar to new realms of personal satisfaction and accomplishment.

As the younger sibling, I observed Jackie's learned skills at our Singer treadle sewing machine and noted how those skills garnered multiple 4-H purple and blue ribbons. Those ribbons were the "carrots" I chased as my sewing skills improved with each garment I constructed. The bar was set high, and I wanted to climb to the precipice of the sewing "windmill," too!

Sewing garments with plaid or striped fabrics could be excruciatingly challenging and frustrating. Pattern pieces had to be pinned to fabric "just so" in order to eventually accomplish matched plaids or stripes throughout the completed sewn garment. I watched Jackie as she and the seam ripper became partners in removing machine stitches that did not allow the plaids to be thread-for-thread matched.

It was a lesson in one of Mom's favorite sayings, "If at first you don't succeed, try, try again!" It was maddening enough to have to keep ripping out stitches in order to achieve sewing perfection. However, when Mom would matter-of-factly speak those words, it was as though hot water was being splashed on to a burn. She did not voice that colloquialism to upset Jackie and, later, me as I was growing in my sewing skills. The wisdom she voiced was meant to serve as words of encouragement for the present situation and for any other challenge life might present.

MY FIRST BOYS' CLUB project was in the form of a steer named Harju (pronounced HAR-u), after the Finnish family from whom the North Ranch (our summer pasture and hay ground) was purchased. Dad helped me train the red Shorthorn steer to lead. At the county achievement day cattle auction in September 1958, Harju was purchased for the amount of $365.75 by Harold Schafer, president of the Gold Seal Company.

After the sale, Mom accompanied me to Mr. Schafer's Bismarck office. He warmly greeted us and made us feel extremely welcome in his presence. As an eleven-year-old country girl, I was in awe of the polished dark wooden walls and rich leather chairs with deep seats. After an invitation to sit across from him at his expansive desk, I felt diminutive as the toes of my shoes grazed the lushly carpeted floor. I worked up the courage to share my personal words of thanks. I had practiced them again and again. This brief pronouncement, "Thank you for purchasing my 4-H steer," was graciously accepted with a smile. He was so kind to show interest in me as a young 4-Her. His warmheartedness has stayed with me my entire life!

Throughout the years, Dad and Mom provided our 4-H steers. The feed was the only expense, and they always gave us a good deal on that, too! The rest of the money went into my college savings fund. Actually, Dad and Mom paid my college expenses, and my 4-H earnings purchased U.S. Savings Bonds, which I cashed in years later to help pay for my husband's and my first house.

Janine

WHEN I WAS SEVEN—far too young to enroll in 4-H—it just didn't seem right that Jackie could show a steer and I couldn't do the same thing!

Even in 1957, I yearned for the experience of feeding and training a steer of my own. I longed to bond with one that was mine—one that Dad had picked from our herd just for me.

Until I was seven, my livestock related experiences with our cow herd and ewe flock were unmemorable. But when Dad picked "Brocky," a brockle-faced Shorthorn steer for my second-grade, non-4-H project, I fed him and combed his beautiful red-haired body as if I were preparing him to be a champion in the show ring! When Jackie's calf was halter broke, so was Brocky. He, too, learned the feel of a leather halter on his head and the gentle tug of the chain underneath his chin when I "asked" him to walk beside me.

Of course, Brocky was never shown. I'm not even certain of his demise. But what I do remember is that this sweet-spirited steer became the catalyst for a lifelong love of cattle, sheep, dogs, and cats, along with a love for the competitive livestock show ring.

"Will 1960 ever come?" I can remember having had this thought about the year when I would finally be old enough to join 4-H. I was thrilled to be initiated into the Menoken Busy Workers 4-H Club during the start of a new club year in the October meeting at Marlys Neugebauer's home. To this ten-year-old, the ceremony seemed quite secretive. Candles were given to each prospective new member. Lights were shut off, making the living room black. The ritual began, and as white candles were lighted, Denice Trauger and I pledged to be dedicated members of our club and "To Make the Best Better" for the benefit of our club, community, and country.

During that era, girls could join a boys' 4-H club and have livestock and crop projects. However, the caveat was that young ladies must also belong to a girls' club through which domestic skills were taught in the required projects of food and nutrition, clothing, and home improvement. Wow! Could my young life become any richer!?! I was then a member of two 4-H clubs! I took to the opportunities 4-H presented as naturally as a duck takes to water!

I WAS FOURTEEN and remember being SO excited that April day when my Pinto mare named Lady had her first foal! It was a beautiful sunny Saturday morning when I looked out the kitchen window toward the pasture and viewed what I thought was a pile of straw next to Lady. I soon realized the pile of straw did not fit into the spring pasture scene—and then the "straw pile" moved! I excitedly ran out to the pasture to greet the new baby. I spent time every day with her buckskin-colored foal, Bucky. Consequently, she was always gentle.

Horsemanship was my favorite project, and Bucky played a huge role in training me to become knowledgeable and skilled in this project. The horsemanship project leader, Kenny Trauger, and Mom (who'd acquired much experience with horses in her youth) helped me tremendously with her training.

After Bucky had grown strong enough to bear my weight, I gently hoisted myself upon her back. To my pleasant surprise, she just turned her head and looked at me and wasn't bothered at all by my location. After all,

Jackie and Bucky, Burleigh County 4-H Halter Showmanship Champion

I'd been grooming her, picking up her feet, and crawling under her all of her life.

Before I put a saddle on Bucky, I rode her bareback. By using this riding method, I learned to become an extension of her and learned how to ride well that way. The partnership progressed to a point where a halter or hackamore was not needed to give Bucky instruction. I just looked and leaned in the direction of travel and used voice commands. Bucky and I had a truly rewarding partnership! Eventually, horse shows and queen contests became a part of my high school and college life.

Jackie was North Dakota Quarter Horse Association Queen, NDSU Rodeo Queen, and North Dakota Rodeo Princess.

MANY "FIRSTS" in my life occurred while in 4-H. The camp experience was one of them. Our 4-H camp was located on the Slade National Wildlife Refuge near Dawson, North Dakota. The two-building facility had been a duck hunting lodge in its former life, but it was perfectly designed for campers.

4-H camp lasted four days and three nights. My first camping experience was when I was eleven years old. It was the first time I'd been away from home for any length of time, and it was my first homesick experience. Being at camp with other 4-Hers was fun, but by the last day, I was ready to go home!

The camp schedule didn't deviate much from year to year. Afternoon and evening activities were my favorites. Splashing in the waters of nearby Lake Isabel was refreshing in the hot North Dakota sun. Yet being in the lake held a negative memorable experience—a blood-sucking leech attached to my ankle! I screamed and yanked it off, causing the skin to bleed. After that, I was leery of going into the lake.

For me, the highlight of 4-H camp was the evening dances, which took place on the baseball diamond amid persistent and omnipresent mosquitoes. Vinyl records were spun on a portable record player. My favorite dance, the Grand March, began the evening fun.

As the music of *Clayton's Grand March,* by Charles D. Blake, resounded through the windblown trees of the campground, we young people of the prairie were far from being in a formal atmosphere, but it felt grand to be in the Grand March if only for a few moments in time.

Janine

FOOD AND NUTRITION was the topic of the required project for Burleigh County 4-H girls in 1960. Another win-win for me! Learning about the science of cooking and baking touched my heartstrings. With each lesson mastered from the required *Beginners' Lesson Book,* I searched the few recipe books that Mom had in her kitchen drawer in order to stretch outside required 4-H learning. The red-checked *Better Homes and Gardens Cookbook* and black, loose-leaf *Martha Bohlsen Cookbook* became my kitchen bibles.

I was attracted to one particular cookie recipe authored by radio home economist Martha Bohlsen—Lace Cookies. Mom had her own activities for the day and was not inside the house to offer advice. Therefore, I ventured onward, gathering all of the needed ingredients, and set out solely to make what I intended to be the most beautiful cookies I had ever seen. However, my novice baking adventure turned out to be a baking disappointment. The batter all ran together on the pan—definitely not a picture of airy lace cookies. Beginning baking experiences are not always successful!

Little did I know that my first 4-H demonstration, Making Muffins, would fit right inside my "toolbox" for my future as a food home economist, dessert creator, and baking teacher. After arranging all of my ingredients and equipment in an orderly manner on our kitchen table like a pro (just as Mom had taught me to do), I practiced and practiced—so much so that Dad never wanted to eat another muffin again!

As the June county contest day approached, I was ready to present to the judge and audience. My head was adorned with a 4-H headband. White apron strings were tied around my waist. I was ready to "rock and roll" with this demonstration. Clothed in the lavender sleeveless cotton top and full lavender print gathered skirt—the result of my first 4-H sewing project—I explained the nutritional value of muffins as ingredients were combined within my cleanly kept workspace.

Even to this day, I can recall the need to keep adjusting the neckline of my blouse during my presentation. As a first-time, ten-year-old 4-H demonstrator, the judge awarded my effort with the overall top award. However, because of my age, I could not advance to district and state competition. I received very valuable constructive criticism from the judge that still serves as a headline of what not

> *4-H members were required to give a minimum of one speech and one demonstration to their club peers each year. Even though I gave many presentations during my nine-year membership, I still felt nervous during the delivery. But as an adult, I realized that these events served as steppingstones to gaining self-confidence in public presentations and performances.*
>
> ✗✪◯ *Jackie* ◯✪✗

to do when giving a presentation: "Try to avoid adjusting your clothing as you are giving your demonstration," she kindly noted on her evaluation sheet.

Up until this point in my life, I was a very shy little girl. As a matter of fact, Mom's full skirts or pant legs served as great barriers between the public and me. But I can truly give credit to the 4-H demonstration program as the impetus for growth and self-confidence.

THE OPPORTUNITIES both Jackie and I had as nine-year Burleigh County 4-H Club members served as the most valuable recipe for tackling the ins and outs, the ups and downs, the I-know-I-can-do-this times of life. With the guidance and teaching of Dad and Mom as we faced each 4-H project's challenges and occasions for personal growth, we learned a valuable lesson in regard to the 4-H motto, "To Make the Best Better." When each of us stepped beyond giving 95 percent of our best and strove for the full 100 percent, rewards of great self-satisfaction accompanied a collection of grand-champion trophies and purple ribbons.

THE SUN'S BRIGHT RAYS reflected off the shiny metal rural mailbox at the end of the driveway. Needless to say, this caught my attention. As

I peered that direction, I noted that posted on a nearby utility pole were two rectangular signs. The message on each was "4-H Club Member Lives Here" painted in green letters on a sparkling white background. I was overcome with joy from the inside out, for the message confirmed in my heart that the breath of 4-H, seasoned with hard work, character building, and family unity, resided on this farm—the Pfeiffer farm.

Menoken Homemakers Club

THE MENOKEN HOMEMAKERS Club was a rural sisterhood. Female "movers and shakers" of our community, including Mom and some of our neighbor women, joined Homemakers. They were wives of hardworking farmers and laborers.

The social custom of using a married woman's first name was beginning to change in this era. Our mother, Mrs. J.C. Pfeiffer, was known as Eudora Pfeiffer in Homemaker records, which also listed Clarice Wachal, Gladys Goehring, Peggy Owen, Zella Trauger, Lois Salter, Marge Perkins, and Maureen Kershaw—just to name a few—who banded together to serve as the "Welcome Wagon" of our farming community. Individually, these women were female family leaders. However, joined together as a team in Club membership, they strengthened the quality of life in our crossroads of America.

In the early 1950s, these women and their families lived without home telephones—probably without televisions either. An invitation to join Homemakers would need to come as a personal invitation, as neighbor reached out to neighbor. A rural woman's experience of the isolation of home was an impetus to join and to invite her neighbors, too.

With membership, our local ladies caught up on neighborhood chatter. They demonstrated their parliamentarian skills when conducting Club business meetings.

The Menoken Homemakers Club was more than an avenue for social gathering. It served as a recipient of long-distance educational outreach offered by the North Dakota State University Extension Service. Women grew in homemaking knowledge for the benefit of their families. Lessons provided by the Extension Service and taught by the Burleigh County Home Extension Agent or Club leaders had a trickle-down, positive effect within our community. After each business meeting, members were coached in the areas of food preparation, safety, and preservation; sewing skills; gardening; health care; refinishing furniture; crafting home décor accessories for added touches of individuality in a family's abode; and a myriad of other topics.

Homemakers were helpmates to their husbands in growing food for their families. Their caring, outstretched arms served as appendages to those community families in need of sympathy or sustenance.

These active volunteers were the citizenry of the approximately ten-square-mile farming area who served as the self-appointed Menoken Chamber of Commerce, charity fund drive organizers, and community betterment group. They were the architects of social life as evidenced by card parties, talent shows, basket socials, Tupperware parties, and community plays.

When it was Mom's appointed month to serve as meeting hostess, we were on-call junior housekeepers. We vacuumed and dusted the house, and eventually set up a circle of chairs around the perimeter of our living room. Mom baked her popular Coffee-Toffee Torte (page 257), set out our rarely used china and silver flatware, and started the club-owned, multi-cup coffeepot to perking. She then garbed herself in a clean, home-sewn, well-pressed cotton dress, high heels, and Tangee lipstick (the fashionable lip color of the era).

A frilly but impractical "company" apron laid in repose in the chest of drawers in our parents' bedroom. But for this occasion—entertaining Homemakers members in our home—Mom retrieved this lovely apron covering from the drawer only moments before the first guest arrived. She wrapped its ties around her slim waist, forming a beautiful self-made bow in the middle of her back. A simple, attached pocket suitably held a flower-embroidered hankie for potential "achoo" containment. This apron was dainty in appearance. By practicality standards, an apron of this sort was off-the-charts impractical. The fabric did not absorb spills, therefore it was poor protection for the garment worn beneath it. A corner of such apron was purposeful in wiping a child's tears yet, due to its fiber content, was incapable of serving as an absorbent holding vessel for dripping nose particles. It definitely was too fancy for transporting green beans and peas from garden to kitchen. It was made of sheer organza and was a beautifully feminine fashion accessory for the modern homemaker of the day but really didn't do much to protect the skirt underneath.

Slumbering in the same drawer that housed Mom's aprons was a stack of beautiful fine cotton handkerchiefs. "Hankies" were not only practical to carry but also served as gifts of kindness inserted between the pages of a birthday greeting card from one club member to another. Often, the fabric had been dabbed with a drop of the giver's favorite perfume which femininely permeated the entire gift. Was it the fragrance of Evening in Paris? Was it the bouquet of Chanel No. 5? It might not have mattered, because the act of giving this lovely remembrance from woman to woman was cherished.

When the Club's progressive supper was planned for New Year's Eve, our house served as the last stop on the supper tour. After dessert was consumed, homemakers and their husbands "cut a rug" in our cement-floored basement as they burned off previously consumed calories. With the aid of our records and single-play turntable, sounds of the fifties—waltzes, polkas, and two-steps—wafted through the heating registers in our bedrooms one floor above the entertainment. It was a time when our parents could put aside the work-every-waking-hour lifestyle and enjoy the camaraderie of friends and neighbors. Dad and Mom were honored to share the lower-level "perk" of our new home—a cement dance floor.

Mom and Dad rarely had the need for a babysitter. We attended community events of all kinds as a family of four. However, there were a few adult events that were planned just for couples, one of which was the aforementioned Homemakers' progressive supper.

The Goehring teenagers, JoAnn and Judy, were community babysitters. Older sister JoAnn Goehring Schrenk was the first to help Mom with our care, but that changed when JoAnn moved to Bismarck as a junior in high school. Soon after that, the Goehrings' cousin, Linda Ehlers Schwengler, joined the Goehring family and replaced JoAnn as one of our babysitters.

At a gathering sixty years later, Judy voiced to Jackie and Janine, "Linda and I used to fight over which of the two of us would come to your house! 'Okay, you babysat for them last time. It's my turn this time!'" Mind you, it was not because we were perfect children, but because, the Goehring cousins later shared, the Pfeiffer house had running water, and the other children for whom they babysat did not.

Janine — MY ABSOLUTE FAVORITE event planned by the Homemakers was the Christmas candy exchange held during the December meeting. I could hardly wait to see all of the colorful homemade candies perfectly positioned on pristine white paper plates! My little fingers eagerly anticipated wandering through the array of yummy candies as my taste buds began to salivate! Marge Perkins sometimes made candy using baked potatoes. With outside edges dipped in chocolate, the candy's center was tinted a jolly Christmas green. Just the thought of potatoes being an ingredient in this delicate little sweet caused consternation in my young taste-testing mind. But her Baked Potato Candy was de-lish (page 258).

For Mom's contribution to the exchange, she traditionally removed the heavy aluminum kettle that had been stashed way back in the corner of the lower kitchen cupboard and made Dad's favorite, smooth and creamy Peanut Butter Fudge (page 260). Dad doted on the sweet square inches of sugary, peanut butter flavor, maybe because he only got to savor them at Christmastime when Mom made an extra batch for the Club's candy exchange.

Marge Perkins, longtime member of the Menoken Homemakers Club, once commented, "My favorite activity of our Menoken Homemakers Club was the county-wide Christmas bazaar. It was a real fancy open house! Two silver coffee services were used. Lace tablecloths were on the tables. We made fancy baked goods for the coffee table. It was an in-house coffee party in a room in the basement of the memorial building in Bismarck. We didn't sell anything. People from all over the county came." The World War Memorial Building was also home to the Burleigh County Extension Office at the time.

When we were youngsters, salads came in varying forms, even if there was not a green leaf in sight. Unless a wedge of iceberg lettuce with Wish-Bone Western Salad Dressing was part of our meal, more notably, a salad was etched in my mind as a wiggly, glassy-appearing intensely colored Jell-O gelatin salad with various fruit additions. Who didn't eat red Jell-O dotted with banana slices or orange Jell-O with crushed pineapple and shredded raw carrots?

By the time we were in high school, Mom had discovered a new way of presenting Jell-O to our family during the holidays. Men's Green Salad made a hit with Dad because it included chopped nuts, cottage cheese, and crushed pineapple, and he definitely was a fan of pineapple! I have absolutely no idea why the title referred to males only. This was never explained to me even though I asked Mom. Not only was this salad prepared for our family, but it became a favorite at Homemakers' events.

THE MENOKEN HOMEMAKERS Club members enhanced the welfare of their families on the prairie and proudly helped their husbands develop our rural population into a progressive, cohesive community.

Mom was a devoted pioneer of this organization during the last half of the twentieth century, as she had joined as a young bride in the late 1940s. When interviewed for inclusion in an oral history project of the North Dakota Extension Homemakers Council conducted by Arlene Sagness, she was asked why she had joined the Club. She stated, "When we first moved here, [being in the Club] was mostly to get acquainted with the neighbors. I think as far as the programs are concerned, there have been good programs all of the time." In 1988, the North Dakota Centennial Commission published the homemakers' recollections in *Sods, Logs, & Tar-paper: Memories of North Dakota Homemakers.*

Chapter 6
Civic Life

WITH MY TEN-MILE proximity to the State Capitol, I easily observed the hustle and bustle of North Dakota government at work. There she stood—Skyscraper on the Prairie—a nineteen-story capitol building, stately, simple, yet fashionably attired in Art Deco form. Clad in Indiana limestone. No glitzy golden spire.

In contrast, Menoken had two places of government—the town hall and the school. The town hall, our one-story civic seat, was humbly covered in white-painted wooden siding and asphalt shingles. The majority governing body of our cohesive rural community consisted of businessmen—farmers, mostly.

Parents of the community's school-age children not only conducted serious PTA business meetings but also concluded the evenings with good-humored social activities.

And food—there was always an abundant spread of food after each gathering!

Wherever my eye could see, the oath of congenial government leadership was followed constitutionally with equal justice for all.

Parent Teacher Association

ON A FRIDAY NIGHT each month during the school year, Dad, Mom, and we girls hopped into the car and drove to our school for a community business/social occasion—the Parent Teacher Association (PTA) meeting. Grade-school children were welcome to attend with their parents. It was a time for the organization's business to be conducted, a sharing of the women's culinary talents after the meeting, and chatter/gossip of farming/homemaking activities.

However, most importantly, this demonstration of how to conduct a business meeting was a teaching tool for us children. We reflected on this display of Robert's Rules of Order many times when we held offices in YCL and 4-H. The PTA experience was another effective example of our parents and community members having influenced our lives for the better.

PTA meetings weren't only about the business at hand at Menoken Grade School. We experienced clean family fun, too! Once a year, a men's night talent show featuring PTA dads presenting side-splitting comedic talents drew hilarious knee-slapping, belly-laughing fun! Dad, Mr. Arntz, Kenny Trauger, Howard Goehring, Paul Hendrickson, Bud Perkins, Arnold Neugebauer, and Ivan Sherman were community fathers who were unafraid to embarrass themselves for the entertainment of their audience. At one program, attired in a red-dyed union suit with an attached red tulle tutu, each gentleman was launched into ballerina stardom!

From left, Jack Pfeiffer, Bud Perkins, and Howard Goehring creating hilarity in a Menoken PTA Talent Show, 1961.

Dad had a celebrated sense of humor! One year, the talent show featured him in the role of hairdresser Miss Fifi. This beautician was determined to get hair to grow on the top of Mr. Arntz's bald head with the aid of freshly cracked raw eggs massaged into her client's scalp! With what little feminine French accent German-bred Dad could muster, he cracked about a dozen fresh eggs on the top of his client's head and tried to sweet-talk hair growth. It was all in vain, though, as not a single sprout of hair began to grow in that time period. Gut-wrenching laughter from both actors and audience filled the room!

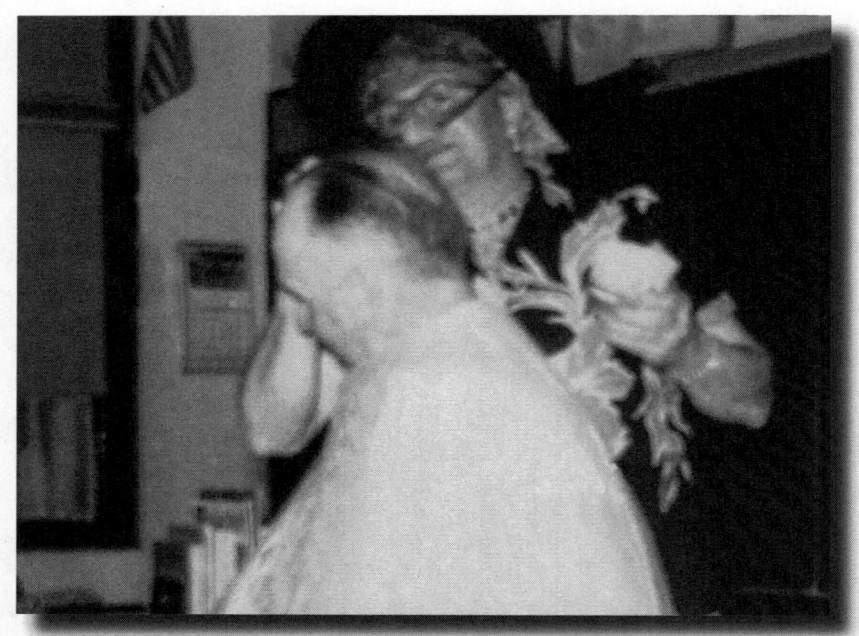

With the aid of raw eggs, Miss Fifi (Jack Pfeiffer) encourages hair growth on the balding head of client Ted Arntz.

Our Parents: Natural-Born Leaders

Janine

MOM AND DAD were compassionate stewards of their land located within the Menoken community. This is where they had chosen to live their lives and raise their family. They had a vested interest in the community, both physically and emotionally.

Although their leadership styles were uniquely different, they were both natural-born leaders. With an unpretentious style, each made worthwhile contributions that helped achieve positive effects in the community.

Citizens favorably cast ballots for Dad during Menoken Township Board elections. He served as its clerk for decades.

Even before Jackie began school as a first-grader, Dad had been elected to the Menoken School Board. Although he toiled far more than eight back-breaking hours a day on the farm, he never tired of adding to this work calendar when community service called. He was following his heart in order to provide input and direction for the education of his children and the children of the entire Menoken community.

THE MENOKEN COMMUNITY

Howard Goehring, Dad's lifelong community friend, and Dad together began as 4-H leaders for the Menoken Progressive 4-H Club and served for almost a quarter of a century. These two gentlemen were bonded together in work and play. People outside of our community also sought Dad to lead county and state livestock organizations.

At the annual 4-H recognition banquet in 1966, Jack Pfeiffer (left) and Howard Goehring were honored for 18 years of service as Burleigh County 4-H leaders. Each would go on to serve several more years.

Mr. Al Bye, our Burleigh County Extension Agent, often encouraged writers from *The Bismarck Tribune* to interview Dad when an active, well-versed voice of agriculture was needed to convey a message to its readers.

In all of the leadership roles and volunteer undertakings Dad fulfilled outside of our family, he served as the voice of the community. As a little girl, I thought that he was the designated leader of the Menoken area!

Mom served for many years as the Menoken School Board treasurer. Our 1950s gray metal kitchen table was her office desk. With an electric adding machine on her right (an upgrade from the hand-cranked one, which was quite a treasured piece of office equipment in that era), she methodically paid the bills of the school district and meticulously made each entry into the hardcover warrant book. She had to be bonded to fulfill this job—a responsibility that was larger-than-life in my little-girl eyes!

Mom was Jackie's and my talented personal 4-H leader for the nine years each of us was involved in the 4-H program. Her lifelong learn-by-doing and do-it-to-your-best character, along with information garnered through Homemakers Club lessons, served as a solid foundation for teaching us the homemaking skills so necessary for women of the 1950s and '60s. This learned competency was a prized library of knowledge when Jackie and I each eventually sought a college degree in home economics education at North Dakota State University.

After I went to college, Mom kept her association with the local 4-H program by volunteering to become an official leader of the Menoken Busy Workers 4-H Club, allowing the young ladies in our community an opportunity to have Eudora Pfeiffer as their mentor. Young seamstresses from other counties reaped the benefits of her knowledge when Mom served as a district 4-H clothing judge.

Additionally, Mom gave of herself in leading the Menoken Women's Society of Christian Service (WSCS), Menoken PTA, Menoken Homemakers Club, Burleigh County Homemakers Council, Burleigh County School Board, and District 5 North Dakota Cowbelles.

Dad and Mom had a vested lifetime interest in the Menoken area. In our adult years, neighbors shared with Jackie and me that our parents were always there for anyone who needed help. With their unpretentious style and caring spirits, they proved to be active leaders within and beyond the boundaries of our community.

YOU HAVE GLIMPSED a slice of the Pfeiffer family's life just as I saw it during the 1950s. The character of Menoken area residents served as the backbone for helping shape the authors' childhoods. Although Menoken was just a tiny stop on the Old Red Trail (Old U.S. Highway 10), it was a giant when it came to growing a cohesive community spirit and legacy!

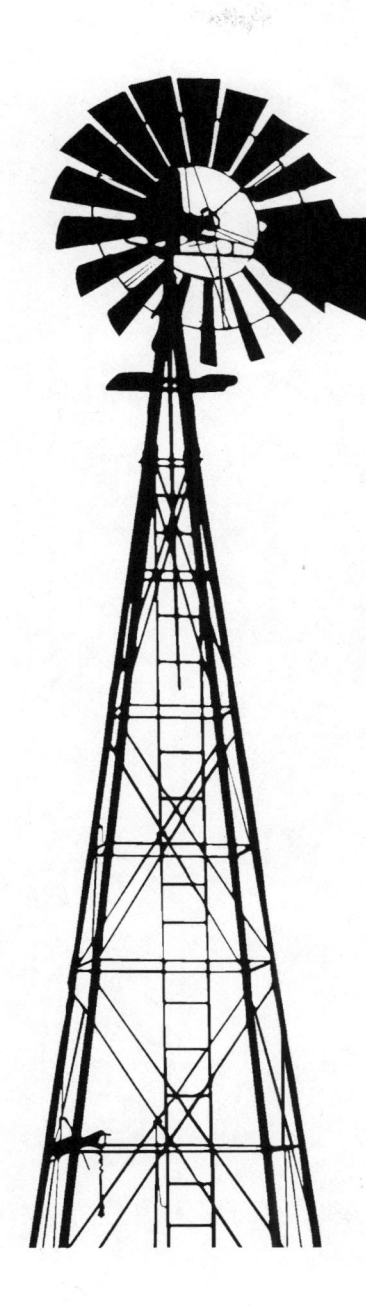

Life on the Pfeiffer Farm

I WAS STANDING stably erect years before Jack and Eudora migrated in 1946 from his parents' farm at Goodrich to their newly purchased section of ground near Menoken. Even though this change in location occurred, just as the prairie wind continually forced the movement of my whirligig, the Pfeiffers' rural lifestyle stayed static.

Admittedly, I observed changes over time—changes that would give rest to the consistent intensity of back-breaking manual labor in caring for the land and livestock. As sands in the hourglass moved within the framework of time, farming became mechanized. Seed and livestock genetics improved. Jack and Eudora sought educational opportunities in order to improve husbandry of the soil and of their livestock.

As you continue to engage yourself in this slice of history, reminisce with Jackie and Janine. They share about special farm animals, learning life skills in the classroom of the prairie, and the all-consuming passion of farming that was a daily companion within their family.

Chapter 7

The Animals

FOUR-LEGGED. TWO-LEGGED. With wings or without. Farm animals represented income. They were the source of home-grown, high-protein sustenance.

Funds from the sale of animals were used to pay the bank, the feed store, and the grocery store. Bills and coins from their sales were traded for fuel purchased to stave off below-zero temperatures. The cream check or egg money paid for children's piano lessons or 4-H project expenses.

Yet, as vital as animals were to the financial bottom line of a farm family, they also provided friendship and camaraderie between man and beast. They gave solace to those seeking a listening ear. Truly, I observed animals as nonprofessional mental health therapists. Stroking a horse's mane or a dog's forehead while sharing the day's woes brought a peaceful regrouping of heart and mind.

Life was simply in balance when a farmer stood within his flock or herd and gazed upon its beauty.

Cattle: Milkers, Feeders, and Show-ers

Jackie

DURING MY YEARS on the farm, our family raised commercial cattle. Generally, these are not purebred in their genetic makeup or registered with a breed association. Commercial cattle are typically sold by the pound at a generic market price established by the commercial beef market. In contrast, purebred cattle sell for much more, because their value is in their purebred makeup, which can be brought to a commercial herd.

Up until about the time when I was in the third grade, Dad milked three or four cows morning and evening. "Moos" greeted Dad in welcome as the cows eagerly awaited the opening of the barn door. Stepping inside the doorway, they hurriedly walked to their assigned places, each moving her head through a wooden stanchion so she could get to the feed that had been placed in front of her.

I remember all of these bovine girls. However, the most notable was a white Shorthorn cow named Snowball. She was an impatient milker, and she needed to wear kickers. Kickers were sort of like handcuffs that were attached to her hocks. If the kickers weren't on, she'd get restless. She'd begin to move around and sometimes kick at the pail, causing the milk to spill, which represented spilled money.

To extract the milk from the teats of the cow's full udder, Dad would balance on a traditional T-shaped milking stool (a two- by six-inch board nailed to the end of a one-foot-long two-by-four), put the pail between his knees, and pull and squeeze a teat in each hand while keeping a hypnotic steady rhythm. The milk frothed in the bucket, the cows contentedly chewed their ground feed, and the barn cats mewed to receive their tasty portion. There was usually one cat that would shut her eyes, hold her head up, and lap the air as Dad squirted the milk directly into her gaping mouth. She'd get her meal and a milk bath at the same time. It was a place of solace in which the tranquil sounds blended with the aroma of manure and hay and cow bodies.

During the milking process, the atmosphere needed to be quiet so that the cows were relaxed enough to let down their milk. I personally don't remember this next situation, but I was told that it was the only time my dad spanked me.

Even as a preschooler, I had music and movement within me! It seemed I just couldn't help myself! But evidently, my singing and dancing were not comforting to the cows. Dad had warned me to be still. Perhaps my joyous actions frightened the cow that Dad was milking, and she inadvertently kicked over the pail, causing the milk to spill!

Uh-oh! Dad was extremely upset with my actions; I knew I was in trouble. I could see punishment coming my way. As I said, I do not remember this occasion. However, in later years, with a little smile on his face, Dad recalled to me that I wanted to negotiate the punishment by saying, "Let's talk about this, Daddy!" It was *not* a negotiable topic. I was punished (but lightly).

Eventually, Dad's arthritis forced him to make a decision—either put money into an automatic milking system and expand the number of cows he currently milked or keep the present milk cows solely as beef-producing females. Regardless of the decision, another income source was needed to replace the weekly milk and cream checks from Schultz Creamery in Bismarck. The milk cows went, and the chicken flock increased!

WE USUALLY HAD AROUND seventy-five head of commercial cows. After April calving, the calves were branded, castrated, and vaccinated. In the late spring, Dad hired several semitrucks to transport the herd to the North Ranch, 960 acres of land that met two different needs—summer pasture for the cattle and hayfield as a source of winter feed.

Once the cattle were back from summer pasture and the calves were weaned, they were penned in the feedlot across from the kitchen window. Mom's heart was warmed by that view, as was Dad's. I have a clear vision of Dad leaning on the white fence of the feedlot, his arms resting on the top plank, just looking at the cattle for the sheer pleasure of it. The curiosity of the cattle would cause them to come close to him to sniff his face and hands as Dad spoke softly to them. Perhaps visiting the feedlot cattle was a way for Dad to "center" himself.

SHE WAS MY FIRST and my favorite heifer. She was solid red in color. Her name was Robbie—my beloved registered Shorthorn heifer. Although we raised various species of livestock, the husbandry of my cattle was my passion!

Janine

I was a young girl when Dad and I selected her from the herd of well-recognized Shorthorn breeder Truman Kingsley, Wheatland, North Dakota. She and I became best companions as I broke her to lead, and I fed, washed, and groomed her for show. Little did I know that her purchase served as the launching pad into my world of livestock production...yes, and eventually to the path of wedded bliss! This passion for Shorthorn cattle was coddled and nurtured on solid ground at our farm.

I desired to learn beyond what Mom and Dad were capable of teaching me about livestock production and cattle showing. Even though my parents did not have the expertise to teach me about this, they supported me with encouragement and finances. They laid the foundation, and then they began to let me soar!

Through the loving kindness of Truman and Connie Kingsley, who took me under their wings, I gained experience in cattle showing at both our Red River Valley and North Dakota State Fairs. This was in the years when livestock trailers did not yet serve as the primary mode of transportation for long-distance livestock travel. Little did my parents or I know when I signed on for the two-week gig that the Kingsley "show string" would make the journey west by rail on the Northern Pacific Line from Fargo to Jamestown, switch railroad tracks to the Sioux Line in Jamestown, and head north to Minot... and it would be a young man, Louie Altringer, and me "roading" them.

The wooden cattle car was bedded deeply with fresh golden straw for the cattle's comfort. Each head of cattle was tied as if in a show barn. Nothing new for cattle jocks...other than we were rolling on a railroad. Cots were provided for us herdsmen. It was an overnight journey with a change of rail line in Jamestown for the northbound trip. Once arriving in Minot the next sunny afternoon, a cattle semi was waiting for us to unload from the train. Destination: cattle barn, North Dakota State Fair. I was unaware at the time that I was experiencing a final piece of history in the transportation of livestock by rail.

What an absolutely memorable stretching experience for this cattle-loving girl! Louie became a very trusted friend. The opportunity to partake in an adventure of such nature was rare. I'm so thankful I unknowingly fell into this chapter in my book of life.

I continued to be a dyed-in-the-wool Shorthorn-cattle enthusiast. During my growing teenage years and eventual collegiate era at North Dakota State University (NDSU), I became friends with people from across North Dakota who shared that same passion. One of those gentlemen was an animal science professor at NDSU, Dr. Bert Moore. He was advisor of the North Dakota Junior Shorthorn Association and mentor to those of us young people who shared the camaraderie of raising Shorthorn cattle. Later in my college life, Bert served as my senior collegiate livestock judging team coach.

The women's auxiliary of every state that had formed a Shorthorn Association sponsored the Lassie Queen contest. Each year the Lassie Queens provided a wee bit of glamour at Shorthorn cattle shows throughout our state and the nation. In 1969, the North Dakota Shorthorn family of breeders titled me with the Lassie Queen privilege. Our Oldsmobile became my carriage of choice as I traveled the state and donned the Scottish Royal Stewart tartan while riding in town parades, making appearances at county festivals and fairs, and handing out ribbons as Shorthorns were placed in show classes.

The honor of representing North Dakota in the national Shorthorn Lassie Queen Contest held at the renowned International Livestock Exposition in Chicago was a highlight of my life. At that show, I was excitedly surrounded by a host of Lassie Queens from many states. The Lassies' enthusiasm for the Shorthorn cattle breed painted a pretty show ring picture. Chosen as a top-four finalist for the national distinction, my joy in representing North Dakota couldn't have been greater!

Janine, North Dakota Shorthorn Lassie Queen, 1969

The Cattle Drive

Jackie

ONE OF THE HIGHLIGHTS of my year was the annual fall cattle drive. It was a pre-dawn-to-after-dark event, a full day in the saddle, often beginning with frost or snow on the ground and ending twenty miles later with frozen phalanges. It was a muscle-aching day. I loved it!

Usually the day before the late-October drive, we'd gather the cow-calf pairs from every corner of the pasture. Dad would call the cows, crying "Come Boss" (pronounced BAHZ). The cattle were corralled, fed hay, and then counted. Dad knew the correct number and figured if there were a few we'd missed in some ravine, they'd find their way to the corral by morning. They usually did, evidenced by a few calves bawling outside the corral the next morning.

The day began at about four, when Kenny and Dennis Trauger drove into the yard towing a horse trailer to indulge in a big breakfast prepared by Mom. With breakfast completed, we'd load my horse, Lady, into their horse trailer and head twenty miles north to the North Ranch.

At daybreak, the first half-hour of the drive was the most frantic! It took that long for the cattle to figure out what they were supposed to be doing. At first, they just wanted to run free in all directions, grabbing the late-season grass as they ran. However, there were always a few older cows who knew the routine. After they'd stretched their legs, they settled down and provided an obedient example that the others followed. We traveled on the county gravel roads and sometimes cut across open fields.

The most irritating thing during the drive was meeting an impatient driver! Invariably, he'd honk the vehicle horn, which made absolutely no sense. Why try to scare the cattle? That wouldn't allow the auto to get through the herd any faster, and it certainly would not make our job easier.

We had been on the trail about six hours when we sighted Mom and Janine in our car, which signaled a welcome rest and dinner. The cows grazed as their calves nursed. We weary humans enjoyed one of the most delicious meals of all time—Mom's fried chicken, escalloped potatoes, baked beans, coleslaw, apple pie, and hot coffee. It was especially tasty because by then the fun of the drive had worn off, and we were cold, hungry, and saddle-weary.

The next hours seemed to drag by. As the day labored on, the tiring calves tended to gather at the back of the herd. Dennis and I were usually the "heelers," those who encouraged the slow walkers. Kenny, who rode the experienced Belle, took care of the occasional rebel cow who might decide to split from the herd on a dead run.

As we neared home, Dad would drive ahead of us in his pickup. He and mom would open the gates to our home corral, allowing the cattle access to water and feed. The older cows sensed the nearness of home and seemed to find a little more energy as we neared it. They needed no GPS guidance. Even in the dark, they recognized our driveway, turned into it, and trotted up the lane toward the water tank in the center of the yard. We usually arrived home about half past eight. The sky was always pitch black, and the temperature was dang cold!

Mom again treated us to a tasty meal, but it wasn't as memorable as the noon feast. I was too tired and stiff from a day in the saddle to care about food; falling into bed was my focus. For Mom, too, it had been a very long day of cooking, as well as doing the morning and evening chicken chores.

Sheep

"HERE, SHEEP, SHEEP, sheep; come sheep" were the repeated words sung out by Dad when he wanted his flock to come to him for one reason or another. Always a businessman, Dad raised sheep because they would potentially yield three yearly sources of income—the sale of the wool, the lamb crop, and the ewes culled for slaughter. He felt a combination of Columbia and Hampshire breeds produced the best blend in wool quality, mothering ability, and abundance of muscle.

There is a well-remembered story by neighbor Judy Goehring Miller that is associated with our brand-new 1957 Buick and our newly purchased ram. The sedan had that new-car aroma. It didn't matter, though; in a few days, that pleasant new-car fragrance would be replaced with a new-sheep perfume! The car was the only vehicle of transportation we had that could efficiently haul a new ram from Fargo to our farm. And that's just what it did! Dad and Mom removed the car's rear seat, laid a heavy canvas tarp on the car's floor, traveled to North Dakota State University, and led our newly purchased registered

Hampshire ram into its green and white carriage. The approximately 200-mile trip west was complete with human and sheep-bleating conversation. The car's interior was thoroughly cleaned after the ram cargo was unloaded. That was the first of many journeys with this motor coach serving as a mode of ram transportation!

We often had bottle lambs. With care given to them, we girls were introduced to the responsibilities of mothering orphaned animals. During the twenty-four-hour day, the lovable little rascals would get their nourishment via a black nipple on the end of a green glass 7 Up bottle. (It was Dad's favorite soft drink, or "pop," as it was known in North Dakota.) Getting up in the wee hours of the night to feed them was a dedicated effort as they needed to stay on a consistent feeding schedule. The little woolly lambs were always glad to see us. As any nurturing mother would do, we not only provided food but loved them with snuggles and soft words. Horace, Oswald, Emmy Lou, and April were the last bottle lambs Jackie and I raised. Horace and Oswald became part of our 4-H sheep project exhibit for that year.

Dad had purchased rams from the renowned Hampshire flock at North Dakota Agricultural College, which later became NDSU. By using these high-quality genetics, it was not out of the ordinary for our young lambs to top the market when sold as either a group of feeder lambs (those just weaned and ready to be fattened with grain and hay) or fat lambs (who had reached a marketable weight of approximately

100 pounds). Therefore, when Horace and Oswald stood at the top of the class as blue-ribbon 4-H fat-lamb exhibits at the Burleigh County 4-H Achievement Show, Dad had as much pride as the breeder of those lambs as Jackie and I had in showing them.

Naturally, bottle lambs became pets, and they would follow us around the yard. Eventually, the lambs would realize they were sheep, and if some of the ewe lambs had been selected to join the flock, they continued to be very tame. One might become the bell ewe and wear a bell around her neck to lead the flock. The bell ewe would come easily when called or when she saw an approach-

Janine and Jackie feeding bottle lambs Horace, Oswald, Emmy Lou, and April 1963.

ing grain-filled bucket in hand. With sheep's natural instinct to stay with the flock, the rest of the ewes would follow.

At Dad's request, sometimes during various lambing seasons, we girls had the opportunity to become novice midwives if a ewe was having a difficult time giving birth. Dad would check the ewe to discern why she was having difficulty lambing. If he realized that the normal birthing position with the lamb's nose resting on both front legs was not present, it was time to intervene. That being the case, the smaller hands of us young girls could fit into the birth canal more easily than his to assist with the birth as nature had intended. It was freezing cold within this outdoor animal science classroom known as the barn. Yet we sisters concluded that using our novice veterinary skills to bring new life into this world was totally rewarding.

The annual sheep shearing event began a couple of months after lambing was completed. Prior to sunset the evening before shearing day, the ewes were gathered in from the pasture and overnighted inside the loafing shed in order to keep the wool dry. Then, at eight the next morning, shearing commenced.

On the appointed June day, a red Ford pickup driven by sheep shearer Mr. Harley Albaugh from Sterling rolled into our farmyard with the tools of his trade. During the shearing of each ewe, he was supported by a sling as he leaned over the ewe. Even with support, his back must have spasmed and ached at the end of the day. Often two additional experienced shearers joined Mr. Albaugh to get the job done within daylight hours. Mom fed the men all day—hot coffee and homemade oatmeal cookies mid-morning, a hearty dinner at noon, and more steaming coffee and cookies about three o'clock.

Shearing took place within the confines of the cool interior of our huge wooden barn. A clean cement floor was of importance for this project because if any tag-along plant material such as hay or straw was included with the fleece, the price per pound received for the wool could be reduced by the wool buyer. "Dirty" fleeces—those with a generous number of weeds, seeds, or plant material—were docked in price by a wool buyer. With broom in hand, Dad stood sentry on the shearing floor, sweeping away any foreign material that could have dropped from the ewe's wool before shearing.

We girls had an important responsibility on shearing day, too. Once the shearer had removed a fleece from a ewe's body, one of us gathered it into a circular wood-slatted bushel basket, tied the fleece with special brown paper twine used for wool, and carried the tied fleece to the young man who was the official wool "tramper" of the day.

Dad usually hired one of his 4-H club boys to help with catching individual ewes for the shearers and with tramping (packing the wool into the sack with a foot-stomping action) the wool tightly into the eight-foot-long burlap gunny sack. The top twelve inches of the sack were folded over the top of the rim of the ten-foot-tall metal piping tripod frame. A levered metal ring was clamped tightly over the top of the frame's rim, encompassing the top of the open burlap sack. Once the sack was tramped full of clean fleeces, the metal levered rim was opened, releasing the full sack of wool. After the two-hundred-pound sack fell to the ground, its open top was then stitched shut with an eight-inch-long curved needle and white cotton twine made especially for this purpose.

The farm truck had another task awaiting it. Multiple filled wool sacks were loaded into the truck's wooden box with the aid of Dad operating the M tractor and Farmhand loader. A few days later, when it was time to sell the wool, Dad shifted the truck into super low gear and proudly drove the truck with its abundant cargo load out of our driveway. Destination: the warehouse location of the Missouri Slope Wool Pool in Bismarck, where a conglomerate of wool producers had joined together to market their commodity to savvy wool buyers. By wool producers "pooling" together to offer a larger quantity of high-quality wool for sale at one time, a higher price per pound was often obtained.

Each ewe was sheared in a time frame of approximately five minutes, then reunited with her lamb(s) in the barn lot. When the final ewe was sheared and reunited with her offspring, Dad opened the corral gate, inviting the ewes to run down the alleyway from the barnyard to the pasture and surround themselves in its green grass. The ewes would quickly get to the business of eating and begin nipping off the stray green shoots of grass even while they were running to the pasture. When we remember this time, we have visions of little lambs frolicking in their newfound freedom.

The personal satisfaction that Dad encountered while watching his freshly shorn flock grazing in the green pasture brought joy and fulfillment to him as a shepherd!

Hogs and Poultry

ALTHOUGH WE were too little at the time to care for the hogs on our farm, Dad and Mom raised Hampshire hogs for over ten years. A bred gilt from Mom's brother, Ray, served as the initial seed stock for the herd.

There is a picturesque memory from our family's hog-raising venture that was imprinted within Jackie's mind. Around the age of two, she accompanied Mom to feed the hogs. It was not uncommon for them to be together to do this. They were standing outside the hog pen. Unaware that Jackie was directly behind her, Mom raised the full slop bucket and swung it behind her to get the momentum needed to swing the bucket over the four-feet-high, solid plank fence. As she swung the bucket backward, it accidentally hit Jackie in the face. Tears rolled down her sweet, previously unblemished face as she cried loudly. The wound was addressed and healed. However, even today, a scar below Jackie's left eyebrow gives evidence of the episode.

Jackie

ONE OF MY FAVORITE DAYS of the year occurred in April when we picked up crates of baby chicks from the Menoken Post Office. When the westbound Northern Pacific passenger train from Bismarck stopped at the Burleigh/Menoken Depot, four cardboard boxes each alive with 50 tiny peeping passengers were unloaded from the mail car. It was a short jaunt across Old U.S. Highway 10 and the tracks for the postmistress, Mrs. Jenny Dance, who gathered the payload of chicks and mail bags. A pleasantly sweet "peep, peep, peep" greeted us as we entered the old stucco Texaco gas station/general store/post office. We two farm girls liked to slide a finger into a small, round air hole and touch the yellow, soft, fuzzy contents.

By July, the chicks would be sporting feathers and wouldn't be as cute, and then they'd be "dressed"—

butchered. We usually decreased the new flock by half, butchering fifty roosters each day for two days in a row. The aroma of wet chicken feathers that seemed to take residence in our nostrils was revolting for several days after.

Janine was always glad to see this day come. She wouldn't miss those aggressive adolescent roosters. When she fed those cocky birds, they often flew at her legs in battle with beaks pecking and talons cutting her legs!

At the time, I did not appreciate that our farm kitchen served as a classroom with Mom as the teacher. Little did I realize that what she taught me about butchering chickens was one of many skills learned in our in-home laboratory that would assist me in my future profession as a home economics teacher.

Poultry evisceration and correct cutting of a whole chicken into pieces was not taught in my collegiate classes. Yet because of what I learned on the farm, I was able to introduce practical knowledge gained from my past to my eighth-grade home economics students in Sitka, Alaska. A student's mother once stopped me at the grocery store and thanked me for teaching her daughter the correct method of cutting a whole chicken into pieces. The student, in turn, had taught her mother. An additional lesson was a cost comparison of a whole chicken versus a commercially cut-up chicken. I am thankful that Mom taught me this unique skill. Thanks, Mom!

OUR FAMILY CLEANED the chicken house weekly on Saturday morning. It was especially difficult for me to rise and shine on dark, winter Saturday mornings. Dad let me sleep until half past eight. Then he'd come to my bedroom door, and he'd softly say, "Here chicky, chicky, chicky!" A few minutes later, he'd patiently repeat it. Then it would progress to "Time to get up, Jackie." I'd stay in bed until the *last* possible second, knowing that by nine o'clock I'd be in the chicken house slinging the manure into the manure spreader with the rest of the family.

Actually, after I went outside and began to help, I enjoyed working with Dad. He was so energetic! He'd tell stories of his youth or talk about who was doing what in the neighborhood or share farm plans; or we'd enjoy a comfortable silence as we worked in rhythm at the task. It was one of those "many hands make light work" times (one of Mom's favorite sayings).

I liked riding on the metal seat of the red manure spreader as it trailed behind the tractor on our way to the barren field. The air was so much fresher there than surrounded by the intense ammonia odor in the chicken house! Someone needed to pull the handle that started the mechanism that moved the manure along the floor of the wagon toward the wide beater that tossed the manure behind the spreader. I was the older and stronger daughter and, therefore, able to trip the mechanism.

Upon our return to the chicken house, baled golden oat straw was spread on the cold cement floor. As evidenced by their "tuck-tucking" and their contented scratching in the fresh straw, they were happy hens!

WE RAISED OTHER SPECIES of poultry for meat—ducks, turkeys, and geese. But domesticated geese (white Emden and gray Toulouse) served many purposes:

- Farmyard alert system/a cacophony of disorganized sound—honking and squawking
- Pillow filler/goose down pillows made by Mom for our family and as wedding gifts made for newlywed friends
- Broom/a feathered goose wing—the tip of which offered a perfect angle for reaching into the corner of each step while sweeping the basement stairs
- Roasted Christmas goose—fresh, never frozen; sold and peddled by Dad to urban customers

- 4-H project exhibit at the Burleigh County 4-H Achievement Days
- Grasshopper-eating posse
- Procreation collection to provide for next year's gaggle

I MOTHERED ONE LITTLE hatched gosling that served as my neck-cuddling pet. His mother chose to ignore the little fellow, who I named Carlos. He was at death's door, but my caretaking of the fluffy gosling imprinted my role of mother in his little mind.

I loved snuggling with him and listening to his "goo, goo, goo, goo" sweet voice. Mom even allowed him to stay in the house with me—at least for a short period of time—until he was old enough to bond with his siblings.

Janine

Horses and Dogs

PRIOR TO AND DURING the dawning years of the 1950s, our team of Belgian horses, Diamond and Victor, was used for all field work. Dad took excellent care of this necessary team of horsepower. A bond of mutual respect strengthened the partnership between man and animal. Dad was dependent upon these work horses for our livelihood. As little girls, we got to ride these gentle giants briefly when they were unhitched from an implement. Dad hoisted each of us up onto a broad, sweaty back. Their never-to-be-forgotten aroma assaulted our nostrils. However, we didn't mind because riding these draft horses was a treat!

We leaned forward with outstretched arms to grasp the silver-knobbed hames, knowing they provided security from falling to the distant ground. The horses then made the round trip to the stock tank for a refreshing drink before being led back to the barn to eat and rest. Dad reminded us to cautiously duck our heads as we entered the barn door. It was an on-top-of-the-world experience!

Jackie, age two, on Diamond

Jackie

I INHERITED MY LOVE of horses from Mom. The first horse that lived on our farm was a pony named Patches. He was a black and white Pinto, the stereotypical ornery Shetland pony. We didn't have him for a very long time before he was traded for Ginger.

Ginger was gentle but still very strong-willed. He wanted to go where *he* wanted to go. He was really too small for me and soon a big horse, Lady, appeared. She was a very gentle mare who had suffered a serious hoof condition called founder, an inflammation of sensitive tissue, the laminae, inside the hoof. My guess is Mr. Arntz, a horse buyer/trader and husband of my grade-school teacher, saved her from the slaughterhouse and sold her to Dad—for a good price.

Since Mom had come from a horse-owning background, I think she might have encouraged Dad to purchase a bigger horse for me. When Lady came into my life, I was in the sixth grade. After school, I would change clothes, grab a snack, and jump on Lady's back. If I'd had a tough day, Lady would listen intently to my rantings and somehow, I'd feel better. One time in my impetuousness, I decided I'd run away from home! I packed an apple and a peanut butter sandwich in a dish towel and hopped on Lady. Most of the time, I rode bareback; it took too much time to mess with a saddle. My covert route was through the half-mile-long south shelterbelt. By the time I'd ridden a quarter of a mile, I somehow felt better. My reasoning kicked in, and I remember wondering why I'd even had such an impractical thought as running away. Besides, it was time to return to do the chicken chores.

MY EXPERIENCE WITH HORSES was less than pleasurable. Ginger, my Ginger. Who was Ginger anyway? He was my rascally ginger-colored Shetland pony gelding. We were bonded together with a love-hate relationship. This Shetland pony was undeniably docile as a kitten but indeed had a mind of his own. Jackie and I crawled underneath his belly and in between his front legs. We slid off his rump. Jackie, who was much more skilled in acrobatics than me, even leaped over his rump in order to ride on his back, emulating the television cowboys! Ginger was nonchalant about all of that. With his velvety nose smelling my outstretched hand, he was always eager to accept sugar-cube treats anytime they were offered.

However, when I wanted to ride this fellow, I'm sure Ginger's testy mental thought process swarmed with self-centered, bullheaded contemplation. He never liked

Janine

to leave home, but, boy did he love to return home! He ran so fast that one might have thought the Wicked Witch of the West was chasing him.

One hot North Dakota summer day, Dad was working in the field about a quarter mile west of our house. Mom had asked me to fetch Ginger from the pasture so that

Jackie on Goldie, Mom on Buttermilk, and Janine on notorious Ginger, 1958

he and I could take a drink of cool water to Dad. Sounds like an easy task, right? Not when Ginger was involved!

I walked out to the pasture, put on his bridle, and tugged him back to the house in order to fetch the jug of water. But after arriving at the house, Ginger would move no further. Mom had no time to deal with a disobedient horse. After she applied a spank to his rump, he bucked, and the light bulb in his brain became brighter. He figured out that it was best to be obedient. He began to trot to the field like nobody's business. That didn't last long, though. Once out of Mom's sight, he downshifted to his favorite gear, trudge-begrudge. I could not get him to move faster to save my soul! As the hands on the clock kept moving, we finally met Dad on the tractor, delivered the water jug, turned around, and headed for home. This Shetland pony of mine immediately metamorphosed from a stubborn stop-and-go pony into a full-throttle trotting/galloping wonder horse.

Ginger was a follower—not a leader. Therefore, when Jackie and I went riding—she on Lady and I on Ginger—he was right on Lady's tail. At times, Lady's equine dietary fumes almost asphyxiated me! Where Lady went, Ginger went! However, if I wanted to ride in a different direction than Jackie and Lady were traveling, it was a no go—which leads me to include the fact that this personality trait of my only mode of transportation at that time triggered the one and only spanking I had ever received!

Recalling that event is an indelible memory! Our closest neighborhood friends, Patty and Janny Salter, lived down "Pfeiffers' hill," across Apple Creek, and a brief jaunt north—only a half mile total. We spent many hours together horseback riding over gravel roads and cutting across dirt paths through our families' farms. We rode bareback most of the time—always with Ginger following Lady. Lady carried Jackie with Janny sitting behind her. Patty sat behind me on Ginger's back as I controlled his reins.

Our baton teacher, Millie McCormick, had recently had a baby. We four were innocently carefree and concocted the idea that it was most appropriate to courteously welcome the little one to our community by visiting mother and child, even though the farm on which Millie's family lived was more than a few country miles from us.

Telephone communication was rudimentary at best in our rural neighborhood. It had never crossed the minds of us four preteens that we should ask permission from our parents to make this trip by horseback. That decision was the genesis of the outcome of the event! Of course, Lady and Ginger served as vital characters in this plot in order to make the round-trip journey of approximately ten miles. The intent with which we made our decision was most caring. However, the problem was that we had not considered that the hour hand on the clock rested at about number four at the time of our departure.

We began our trip by walking our horses out of Salter's driveway and heading north on the gravel road. This was to be somewhat of a casual jaunt—we thought. We had no more than ridden a few hundred feet when Patty and I had second thoughts about continuing on with our travels. She and I decided to turn around and ride back to Salter's farm. However, we hadn't consulted Ginger about that decision. Realize, again, that Ginger was a follower and not a leader; therefore, he was not about to let Lady out of his sight. If he could have been a bumper sticker on Lady's hindquarters, that would have been his chosen lot in life.

I pulled on the reins to stop him from moving forward, with the expectation that my skillful guidance would turn him 180 degrees in the opposite direction. He followed my command but made only a quarter-turn into the middle of the road, planted his four feet into the gravel, and abruptly stopped! We stood crosswise in the middle of the road. Patty and I dismounted from the cantankerous steed, pulled the reins over his head, and expected to move the horse by coaxing him with kindness. He had made up his mind; no amount of "sweet nothings" was going to cause him to casually walk away from his sidekick, Lady! Ginger was belligerent, and Lady and her riders continued northbound. Either Ginger, Patty, and I remained in the middle of the road and possibly got run over by an oncoming vehicle, or we needed to remount my steed, catch up with Lady, and ride onward on my pony, realizing that I might eventually face a potential disciplinary outcome. Patty and I made a grave decision! The only way for Ginger, Patty, and me to be safe was to move out of the middle of the road by "rewinding" Ginger in a reverse quarter-turn so that Lady was in his sight. He then was ready to run as fast as he could to catch up with his equine friend. Patty and I quickly climbed aboard the rascally fellow and galloped right up to Lady's tail and then quietly continued on with our two-horse, four-rider trek.

This might seem like it was the best decision on the part of Patty and me as we four equestrians/baton twirlers then accomplished our goal to greet the new babe and mother. Realize, though, the late summer sun was setting in the west, and darkness was rolling in while we were at Millie's house. We were still miles from home. Stars began to twinkle in the Heavenlies, which helped light our road home. As our caravan reached a point at which we could ride a mile across the dirt path of Salter's field, we reached Patty and Janny's house, they dismounted, and Jackie and I continued south, walking our horses for the final half-mile in our round trip.

Little did we know that Mom had been worried sick about the whereabouts of her daughters and their horses! The trepidation in my heart in regard to our whereabouts associated with the time of day was proven true. When we arrived home, Mom walked out of the house, meeting us in the barnyard. I had just swung my leg over Ginger's back in order to plant my two feet on the ground beside him when three determined swats to my derriere were administered! They weren't administered lightheartedly either. Mom meant business! Amidst my tears, I tried to explain the situation to her and offered my excuse of Ginger having been the true culprit in this saga and that she should spank Ginger! However, after our one-sided "discussion," her only words were, "Now, take care of that horse!"

It's interesting the vivid memories that still occupy my mind. It was almost ten o'clock. The program *Cannonball* was on the television when I somberly walked into the house. The aroma of liver and onions, one of Dad's favorite meals, permeated the kitchen. Mom was not an abusive disciplinarian. The level of her discipline paralleled her level of love and concern for her children. In this situation, I had been in a quandary in my young decision-making process. Do I listen to my horse, or do I listen to my conscience? I listened to the horse and made a wrong decision. This blip on the radar screen of my life was an unusual circumstance that to Mom's way of thinking required an unusual mode of discipline. The consequences of my having made a potentially erroneous decision still influence my life.

With such a stubborn mount, it didn't take long to realize that my preferred childhood mode of transit on the farm and local gravel roads was astride my brand-new blue-and-white bicycle, Blue Boy. I was with Mom and Dad when they purchased it from Bismarck's Montgomery Ward store for my seventh birthday. In comparison to Ginger, when I swung into that brown saddle seat, no complaints followed. The wheels turned every time I pedaled them. I loved Blue Boy! Ginger probably did, too, as I no longer interrupted his lingering days of pasture-grazing splendor.

ALL OF OUR DOGS were named Shep. The first Shep came from Grandpa Wiese, Mom's father, when I was age three. He joined Scotty, an old, short-haired, spotted dog that seemed to always have flies around his face as he walked on unsteady legs. He wasn't very endearing. He probably came with Mom and Dad when they moved to the farm from Goodrich.

I played with Shep when he was a puppy, but he soon became Dad's companion, and therefore Dad's dog. Dad, who was a tenderhearted man, felt so badly when Shep died. Shep had eaten some docked lambs' tails that had been collected in a pail after removal and had not yet been properly discarded. Shep's death was due to his inability to digest the tails. It must have been painful for the poor dog! It was the first time I had seen Dad cry.

Through the years, a plethora of dogs lived on our farm, with the last two being Border Collies. They were smart dogs, and Dad delighted in watching them work.

Chapter 8
The Equipment

A FARMALL M TRACTOR thrust our farm into the labor-saving world of mechanization in 1950. In lieu of equine horsepower, this tractor furnished a huge leap in pulling power when using a variety of field implements. In addition, the tractor proved to be the foundation for the Farmhand hay bucker, fork/hay loader attachment; the sturdy steel manure fork; and the broad, deep snow bucket.

A 1952 INTERNATIONAL Harvester farm truck—blue cab with mounted red wooden grain box and removable white cattle rack—served multiple purposes. Some trucks, like

Janine

ours, had the added luxury of having a hoist to raise and lower the box for ease of dumping its contents.

It even sang—at least the simple, wretched heater inside the cab did! From inside the heater's metal belly, it produced a tumultuously mournful noise—screechy and high-pitched with a tremulous vibrato. It cried its little heart out, producing more noise than heat. However, that wee bit of warm air did prevent us from freezing as we traveled hither and yon across the frigid prairie. Our truck stood ready for work—at least when it would start!

Dad and Jackie, age three, picking corn, 1950

As our home was heated with North Dakota lignite coal, our farm truck transported the coal to our home. When Jackie and I had an invitation from Dad to accompany him to the coal mine, we hurriedly donned our warm chore clothes and climbed into the truck's cab.

One late fall destination was a coal mine north of Bismarck. Once our truck's box was loaded with large chunks of coal, we began the drive home. The homeward journey was exceptionally slow going due to the heavy load of coal. At best, the truck's speedometer registered forty miles per hour. Without a radio broadcasting farm markets, music, or chatter (and there being no seat belts in the truck in the 1950s), Jackie and I often turned on the bench seat to face backward and sing to our reflections in the cab's rear window. "We're going backwards! We're going backwards!" This creatively simple sing-song chant combined with the heater's mournful howl must have been a joyful noise to Dad. He never requested that we girls stop the music, turn around, and sit still. After all, he was with his girls—and he loved that!

Finally, we approached the welcome sight of our farm's driveway. Dad backed the truck up to the west side of our home, opened the black iron coal door to the basement, and engaged the hoist that lifted the truck box. After the box's endgate was opened, the coal was guided by a makeshift wooden chute as it rumbled into the contained coal room. The luxury of having a hoist made certain that the only manual labor Dad produced in this process was to clean up the bits and pieces of coal that were hiding in the corners of the wooden truck box. A supply of fuel for our furnace ensured winter's wind chills would not capture us!

I was Dad's farming buddy. In the summer, I rode with him in the cab of our farm truck, the box loaded with recently combined wheat, to deliver it to the privately owned Menoken Elevator. It was a short, three-mile jaunt. Upon arrival at the elevator, we waited our turn in the line of farm trucks and tractors pulling grain wagons. As the wheat unloaded into the elevator pit on these parching late-summer days, Dad would reach into the pocket of his denim blue overalls and produce two dimes for us to purchase chilled refreshment from the pop machine located in the Elevator office—7 Up for him, orange pop for me. It was our daddy-daughter date, of sorts.

We were dryland farmers; no irrigation pivots were necessary. The wheat grown on our farm was usually custom combined. Before any wheat was harvested, we watched Dad ream a head of wheat in the palm of his hand, chew a few kernels in his mouth, and determine if it was ready to be harvested. Mom taught us how to produce wheat gum with ripe kernels by masticating about a teaspoonful with our teeth and jaw. "Don't swallow the wad! Keep chewing, and you'll make a wheat gumball!"

Unlike the wheat, Dad harvested the vast oats field pulling our Gleaner Baldwin combine behind the Farmall M. The deep-throated sound of the combine's

Dad, Janine (age 12), and Mom in a beautiful oats field, 1962

motor indicated it was ready to thresh the grain, which would eventually be stored in our wooden granaries and used as feed for cattle, sheep, and poultry.

BEING AROUND OATS made my skin itch! Inhaling the dust made my nose and chest plug up. But when Dad needed a driver to move our farm truck closer to the combine for eventual dumping of grain, I was the dedicated underage driver. What farm kid didn't know how to drive a vehicle before the lawful driving age?!

> *The granaries offered enticement in the form of a small sea of slippery golden grain in each partitioned room. But I didn't dare jump into that attraction! Dad was a stickler for safety. I'd been warned that a child could drown in temptation, in this case, physical temptation!*
>
> ⨯⨯ *Jackie* ⨯⨯

One might think that this was a boring job for me. No sir, no ma'am! Here's the reason: the Bismarck Woolworth's on Main and Fourth Street had a great selection of *The Bobbsey Twins* books by Laura Lee Hope that I had purchased for summertime reading. The truck cab served as my reading library room.

Boredom was avoided. When Dad gave a giant "come over here" hand wave, it was time to start "the old gal" (as he called the truck), gently drop the clutch with my left foot, give 'er some gas with my right foot, and drive across the straw stubble to meet the combine for a grain dump.

Through our farming years in the mid-twentieth century, additional farm equipment was updated that led to more advanced farming practices. Dad's diagnosed osteoarthritis played a dominant role in his ability to farm. He overlooked the burdening pain in his joints and doggedly worked in the farming life he loved in spite of the debilitating pain. Rather than joyfully running from task to task, though, he now was resigned to a rapid, determined walking cadence.

DAD AND MOM'S PARTNERSHIP evolved from horse-and-buggy days to the almost unfathomable feat of a man walking on the moon and beyond. In that time frame, farming became mechanized. Overall, it was profitable and truly satisfying to their entrepreneurial spirits. After retirement from active farming, Dad reminisced with his son-in-law, Fred Knop, and fondly relayed, "I lived in the best of times!"

FROM WHAT YOU HAVE JUST read, you now understand the attachment the Pfeiffers had to their rural environment. The passion with which Jack and Eudora gave of themselves to farming was only magnified by their conscientiousness in planting deep family roots within the lives of Jackie and Janine.

Chapter 9

The Weather

INTENSE HEAT! FRIGID COLD! Unabating wind! Pelting snow! Torrential flood! Over time, my four-legged metal framework expanded and contracted with these day-to-day, dissimilar climatic changes on the prairie. The accompanying devastation of these natural events to the land, livestock, and people periodically served as evidence of the sky's sovereignty over the prairie.

In contrast to weather's havoc, the northern Great Plains often portrayed exquisite scenic beauty. As I felt the refreshment of slowly falling raindrops from heavenly skies and inhaled ozone's cleansing aroma, the parched soil sang a welcome relief. Beautifully colored western horizons and high-arched rainbows applauded in scenic appreciation. The sight often took my breath away.

Jackie

THE WEATHER ORCHESTRATES a farmer's schedule throughout the year. In the early 1950s, the North Dakota meteorological conditions were still living up to their reputation for extremes—very cold in the winter, very hot and sometimes humid in the summer, and always windy. In fact, I once heard that, on the average, there were only thirty days out of a year when the wind did not blow in North Dakota! I remember Mom often saying, "I hate this incessant wind!"

The combination of snow, low temperatures, and wind created problems for Dad and our livestock. For a child, it created possibilities. One day, excitement came in the form of a circling airplane. I was about five years old, but I still remember that the mail fell from the sky in a canvas bag! Evidently the county road had been closed for some time due to an abundance of snow. In dropping the mail from an airplane at each rural township residence, the U.S. Post Office executed its familiar motto: "Neither snow nor rain nor heat nor gloom of night stays these couriers from the swift completion of their appointed rounds."

The prairie winter brought harsh, wind-whipped, driven snow that formed mountainous snowbanks. The calm after the storm resulted in a crisp, crunchy carpet embedded with a crust of diamonds. Taking a deep breath of the pristine air, I could feel the nostril hairs in my nose freeze.

I am reminded of this when looking at a photo of me at age two holding my doll, Sissy, tucked under my arm. I'm standing on a snowbank, stuffed into a snowsuit, and wrapped up with a wool scarf around my neck. I felt so

Jackie on a snowbank, with doll Sissy

swaddled that I could hardly move! Mom once told me that it would take her five minutes to get me ready. I'd be outside for about five minutes and then want to come in because I was already cold with rosy red cheeks and frozen fingers and toes.

I loved being outside with Dad—or anywhere with Dad, for that matter. I recall one winter when there was so much snow that he could not use the tractor to transport hay to a feedlot. Dad hitched the team of Belgians, Diamond and Victor, to the big sled that had the attached hayrack.

It was fun to ride on top of the hay with Daddy! It was almost like floating on a cloud. I could see forever at that level! All through my life on the farm, Dad was always very conscientious about alerting me to possible danger around machinery or animals, or in other situations. In this instance, he warned me to sit right beside him and not play around on the hay. Thus, I was near him when the sled got stuck in the snow. For some reason, the hayrack gently tipped to the right side with a thin blanket of hay, Dad, and me following. In slow motion, we collectively slid from the top of the hay to the top of a snowbank. I thought it was fun and just a little scary!

In thinking of this event, I realize that it just added to Dad's workload. Dad and Mom worked as a team unhitching the horses, removing the remaining hay from the rack, digging the sled out of the snow, and repositioning the hayrack onto the sled frame. With pitchforks in hand, they reloaded the rack, rehitched our team of horses to the frame, and delivered the load to hungry livestock in the feedlot.

One time and one time only, I had an intimate experience with the metal frame of the windmill. Anyone who has experienced a North Dakota winter has probably been warned that it's best to admire frost-on-metal from a distance. In other words, keep one's tongue in one's mouth! Do not attempt to lick frost off a metal object. Dad had warned me to not yield to temptation of many kinds, and licking frost on the windmill frame had been one of those warnings. I thought the frost would feel fuzzy on my tongue. Of course, I had to try that. I did it just once! Through Dad's chuckling, he showed empathy by pumping water from the well into a metal cup that consistently hung by a short wire on the windmill frame. My attached tongue was loosened from its intimate bond with the metal as Dad dribbled chilly water over it.

Too Much Water

Jackie

DURING THE 1950s, North Dakota rivers and creeks often flooded in late March or early April. Severe floods generally followed winters of heavy snows.

I was five years old at the time memorable flooding occurred in 1952. The winter snowpack yielded an exceptional amount of water. Apple Creek meandered through our pasture on its way to the Missouri River, allowing its flood waters to spill into our pasture and over the county road.

The KFYR Radio Tower Station was our pasture's next-door neighbor. The overflowing creek prevented Bismarck employees from driving to the station building. For several days, they parked their cars at our farm, and Dad hitched the team of horses to the hay wagon and "floated" the men back and forth to work each day until the water receded.

It was due to a kindly KFYR employee, Mr. Gorder, that I experienced my first taste of a bologna sandwich. Wow!

That first bite startled my taste buds! Salty processed meats were not a part of our farm diet!

One of the most historic weather incidents on the northern Great Plains occurred in March 1966. I was a student at North Dakota State University and had finished my finals early. I had hitched a ride west with other students, arriving at home as the horrendous "Blizzard of '66" was assaulting the prairie! In retrospect, the car in which I had been riding must have been one of the last ones traveling on Interstate 94 before the effects of the blizzard closed the highway.

Similar monstrous blizzard conditions have been described in books such as the Little House book series by Laura Ingalls Wilder. As in descriptions found in "pioneer books," Dad actually ran a rope from our house to the cattle tank beneath the windmill so that he could periodically break the ice for the animals in the feedlot. Unfortunately, the range cattle were not as fortunate. The phrase "You couldn't see your hand in front of your face!" was apt.

The blizzard raged for three worrisome days, invading a large part of the state! During those hours it dropped twenty to thirty inches of snow, with the highest snowfall recorded as thirty-eight inches. Wind gusts reached more than seventy miles per hour, creating tremendous snowdrifts that covered the tops of some mature trees in the shelterbelt.

Years later, neighbor Marge Perkins recalled to Janine and me that Mom had been so concerned about her family's well-being in southeastern North Dakota after the dangerous furor had passed. Having lost phone service to our home, she put on layers of outdoor winter clothing and valiantly fought frigid temperatures and mountainous drifts of snow as she trudged on foot over a mile to the Perkins's farm in order to use their working telephone.

Even though the Perkins family's phone service was with a different company, Mom had no assurance that it would be in service upon her arrival. She needed affirmation that her family was safe. Gratefully, the phone

Near Jamestown, North Dakota, on March 9, 1966

was in working order, and the message heard from the phone's receiver reassured her.

When the eerie stillness after the blizzard finally came upon the prairie, so did the discovery of the devastation that had been left in its wake. In a futile attempt to escape the strong, harsh north wind, our cattle and sheep had drifted a half-mile to the southernmost fence line. The animals were snow-blind, confused, hungry, and thirsty; some were dead. Many dotted lumps of snow marked where the weak had fallen. The eyes of the living animals pleaded for help. Some animals had frozen feet, which resulted in them being put down. The suffering of the animals was so, so very sad! Even some animals that were not in the open did not escape death. A neighbor lost all of his heifers that were inside a large pole barn because the roof collapsed on them. According to reports, the storm was responsible for the deaths of 112 people and more than 74,000 cows, in essence obliterating the open-range cattle industry in the state.

The Senses of Weather

THE SCENT OF THE AIR when rain was falling on the dry earth was as if God had sprayed the air with cleansing freshness! The rain was a welcome blessing before and after crop-seeding time; it was a curse during harvest when the grain needed to be dry. The hail was not welcome at any time, because of the potential damage to a standing crop.

When thinking of a North Dakota sky, two scenes come to mind.

The first is the nighttime prairie panorama that occasionally was on fire with colorful Northern Lights (Aurora Borealis) showcasing lightning-strike color! The prairie was alive with the Lord's energetic paintbrush! This heavenly, brilliant kaleidoscope of color served as prelude through postlude of a winter prairie symphony, contrasting with a canvas of peaceful, whitewashed, pristine snow. "Come to the motion picture show," called the late-night sky. "Open to the public. Admission FREE!"

The second recollection consists of big, white, fluffy cumulus clouds, sometimes suspended, sometimes sailing across the royal blue expanse above the horizon.

Occasionally at dusk, pink and blue "ice cream" clouds evoked the feeling of contentment. (The clouds looked more like cotton candy, but "ice cream" is the term that stuck within our family.) After Dad had come in from the field, the chores were done, supper had been eaten, and the dishes had been washed, our family often sat on the front steps in the heavy summer air. We watched the clouds and the distant streak and heat lightning as we listened to the far-off rumble of thunder. Sometimes this contented scene evolved into dark storm clouds that produced light or heavy rain, or even hail.

Nevertheless, while snuggling next to Mom and Dad, a contented feeling resulted from the realization that we were swaddled in safety! We were enrobed in love!

COULD YOU FEEL IT—the chill-to-the-bone blizzard wind? Did you see it—those colorfully painted North Dakota skies? Weather was at the apex of the Pfeiffers' farm life. These rugged folks were immersed in their ability to adapt to change due to varying weather situations.

Chapter 10
The Chores

THE PFEIFFER FAMILY operated as a team. Jack and Eudora worked cohesively, breathing a strong work ethic into the lives of their children. The bloodlines of their ancestors had introduced that virtue decades previously.

Chores required of The Sisters were not difficult. But what the responsibility of those chores fostered was both personal and family accountability. Teamwork! Year in and year out, "Working Together" was the unspoken mantra on the Pfeiffer farm.

EQUAL OPPORTUNITY was alive and well on the farm. Dad didn't have any sons, but that didn't matter to him. Janine and I had the best of both

Jackie

worlds because we had the opportunity to learn skills from both Dad and Mom. One time I asked Dad if he was sorry to not have had sons. He replied, "I'd rather have daughters. If I had sons, the government probably would just send them to war." Besides, our contribution to the farm was no less than a boy's contribution would have been.

Both parents were very energetic! Before Dad's arthritis slowed him down, he would either walk very fast or run across the yard going from one task to the next. When Janine and I were helping him and a tool was needed, we'd run to the shop or to the garage to get it and run it back to him. We ran because we knew there was much to do during the day, and Dad's time was precious!

> *When thinking of the value of chores, we are reminded of the Fruits of the Spirit as listed in Galatians 5:22 "...love, joy, peace, patience, kindness, goodness, faithfulness, gentleness, and self-control."*

Dad did believe in rest, however. During field work, he would come to dinner around noon; eat while listening to the farm market news; then lie on the floor for a fifteen-minute nap. (Our house didn't have air conditioning, and it was cooler on the floor.) He believed in a time of rest on Sunday as well.

Outdoor and inside chores were very much a part of our upbringing. A farm family must work together as a unit in order to achieve agrarian success, and work we did! Janine and I were expected to do our part; the degree of responsibility increased as we matured.

One time I asked Dad for an allowance. "Why do you need an allowance?" He imparted that if I continued to work as a family member, he'd give me anything that I might need. I deciphered the meaning of the message as I'd be supplied with what I needed and not necessarily what I wanted, and the subject was closed. On the other hand, Dad was always more than fair and generous, and sometimes I did receive a desired want.

Indoor chores consisted of vacuuming, dusting, cleaning the bathroom, setting and clearing the table, washing and drying the dishes, ironing, doing the laundry, and helping Mom with the canning, freezing, baking, and many other duties that were a part of the smooth functioning of a farm home.

When I was about eight years old, I started to learn the skill of ironing with Dad's red and blue bandana-print work handkerchiefs. Eventually I had honed my technique well enough to avoid leaving an occasional wrinkle in the hankie and advanced to the next level of ironing, his special white handkerchiefs. In today's society, a man might be more apt to use a disposable paper tissue rather than a cloth handkerchief. After that, I progressed to pressing Dad's denim shirts and finally to his dress shirts. My first 4-H demonstration when I was ten was the correct way to iron a shirt. I had experienced lots of previous practice! It is of interest to us that when pressing our husbands' shirts, both Janine and I still maintain the standard of pressing the entire shirt, even though, at times, only the collar and cuffs are exposed when topped with a sweater.

One of my first ironing experiences wasn't very pleasant! It happened on a summer Friday morning as our family was hastily preparing for an all-day egg-delivery trip to Bismarck. Mom had washed my favorite summer top—white with red and blue rick-rack trim. I wanted to wear it to town that day, and Mom hadn't had time to iron it. I was an independent six-year-old and willfully thought, "Okay, I'll do it myself!" I can still see the horizontal burn scar on my rib cage today. I finished ironing the top and wore it that day with a mixture of chagrin and pride, along with a bandage over my blistered skin.

Not everyone can list this next skill on their resume: cleaning a cream separator. Because of my eight-year-old stature, it was impossible for me to lift the heavier of the two metal bowls that contained the fresh cows' milk. When it was time to clean both bowls, Mom transferred them to the nearby deep sink, and I took over the chore. The personally satisfying part in the process was scraping out the ring of scum inside the smaller bowl with my index finger. My goal was to have that scum ring leave the bowl in one complete circular piece—like a halo. When it did, I felt true accomplishment!

Our outside chores were vast, helping with all aspects of gardening, from planting the seeds, to weeding, to harvesting; feeding and watering the chickens and gathering the eggs throughout the year; feeding our 4-H lambs and steers; and tossing grain to the geese, ducks, and turkeys.

The safety of the chickens was extremely important as they provided our source of weekly income. The hens naturally congregated inside their house at dusk. All Janine and I had to do was run outside and shut the door. This kept predators—skunk, fox, or raccoon—from invading the roosting layer hens. The safety of our cage-free hens wasn't important only at night but during the day as well. Chicken hawks (merlins) were known to dive-bomb our hens in broad daylight. When the chickens spotted the airborne enemy, they ran for cover!

DID YOU WALK side by side with Jackie and Janine as they did their chores? It might have seemed repetitious—even I thought so as I watched them day after day. It took the cooperation of each family member doing their part in order to make the Pfeiffer farm prosper. What was the crowning accomplishment of all that responsibility? The building of ethical character and discipline in the minds and hearts of Jackie and Janine.

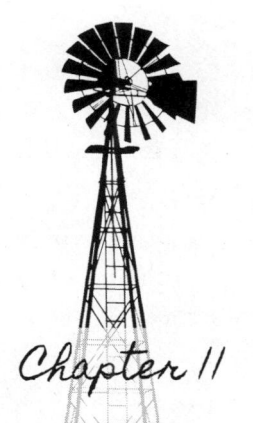

Chapter 11
Preserving the Bounty

WORK ON THE PRAIRIE by both male and female was demanding of a body. Fresh water and fuel-producing food anchored the body's battle cry for replenishment. The Pfeiffer family stewarded their crops, livestock, and garden to gain maximum production for sustenance. And then the designated bounty was harvested and preserved to last for months.

A home deep freeze was packed full of beef and chicken, along with Eudora's baked goods, while a basement-level "fruit room" contained shelf after shelf of pint and quart jars of home-preserved jams, jellies, fruits, pickles, vegetables, and meat. Whether blizzard, flood, drought, or blistering temperatures, I know for a fact that year after year, the Pfeiffers made certain that their larder was filled!

Jackie

FOOD PRESERVATION occurred sporadically throughout the calendar year—canning and freezing fruits and vegetables, making pickles, and butchering beef, turkeys, ducks, and geese.

Mom's very large garden near the house produced a plethora of vegetables and berries as well as chives for a German dish we called *schnittlauch*—chives mixed with creamy cottage cheese.

It was so soothing to have our bare feet caressed by the warm sandy loam soil of the garden—until the heat from the soil became unbearably uncomfortable! The parching summer sun that took residence over the northern Great Plains rarely gave outdoor workers a reprieve. Yet, going shoeless was often our foot-fashion standard while gardening.

Dad's cousin, FBI agent Alvin Schlenker, occasionally brought gifts from his latest worldly destination to us girls. One summer upon returning to Bismarck to visit his parents, he brought straw hats from Jamaica. Our gifted gardening attire kept the sun off our faces as we weeded and watered the growing plants.

Gladiolas (Mom's favorite flower), iris, dianthus/pinks, marigolds, and bachelor buttons greeted those who entered her garden. A large, fragrant yellow rose bush occupied one corner of the garden. No matter what the growing season, intentional plants and ubiquitous weeds both excelled in the rich North Dakota soil!

Flowering along the south perimeter of the garden were bushes that featured an added bonus. While performing the mundane work of weeding the garden, the heavy fragrance of flowering lilacs wafted across our farmyard in May. Throughout my life, the aroma of lilacs—my favorite flower—still reminds me of home.

Janine and I learned to "put up" (the term used by Grandma Pfeiffer) or to can and freeze a cornucopia of products. We helped Mom make several kinds of pickles—dill, sweet, chunk, bread and butter, watermelon

Jackie and Janine, gardening in their Jamaican straw hats, 1961

pickles, and beet pickles. The garden vegetables were either canned or frozen or both. Mom occasionally made sauerkraut in a large crock in deference to our German heritage.

Janine — AS JACKIE AND I grew in years, preparing sweet corn for the freezer became a family affair. In the cool of the morning, Dad and Mom would drive out to the field to pick the ears from the stalks. Jackie and I would have to arise by the time they brought a pickup load up to the house. Then, as Mom got the supplies and tools necessary to preserve sweet corn, we girls joined Dad in the husking and silk-removing process. While Mom commandeered the activities of blanching and shocking the ears with ice, we other three became experts at removing sweet corn kernels from the cobs. Towers of freezer bags filled with this naturally sweet vegetable were soon laid to rest in our massive chest-style deep freeze. Yes, it was work, but Dad and Mom taught us the value of working as a family team for the better of us all.

AN EXCEPTION TO A MORNING sweet corn processing occurred one August evening. During the summer, we usually ate supper after dark because Dad worked in the field until dark. At that time of my life, my bedtime was nine o'clock. I was lying in bed, but more work was still being done in the kitchen. Mom and Dad had been up working since sunrise, and while I was preparing to rest, they still worked for three more hours after supper! The sweet corn was ripe; letting it ripen for even another day might cause it to become too tough. It needed to be preserved immediately. That incident is one of many that made me realize and appreciate my parents' industriousness.

Jackie

WE CANNED A VARIETY of fruit even though not all of it was grown in the many rows of trees that surrounded the farmstead. Mom and Dad purchased wooden flats of peaches, pears, and Bing cherries (our favorite), and we canned these fruits in light sugar syrup.

The north shelterbelt offered crab apples and chokecherries. I loved the candied cinnamon crab apples that Mom made. The chokecherries as well as the strawberries, gooseberries, and raspberries became jam.

As was usual for farm homes of the 1950s and 1960s, air conditioning was uncommon. The air currents in our hot house were disturbed by a couple of floor fans that circulated the hot air that had blown in through widely open windows. Still, when Mom had turned on all four burners of our gas range to begin canning and preparing to freeze fruits and vegetables, the thermometer's mercury rose exponentially in the kitchen!

In August, Johnny and Ella Zimmerman (Dad's sister and her husband) made the ninety-mile trip from Jamestown to pick chokecherries. In return, Johnny would give us some chokecherry wine in December. Nevertheless, a five-gallon carboy—a glass vessel used in fermenting fruit—occupied space in our basement for just a few years when Dad briefly traded his farmer straw hat for that of a vintner. He discovered that the quality of his wine wasn't up to par with Johnny's, so his career as a vintner was short-lived.

In November and December, we processed ducks, turkeys, and geese. Dad took orders from his "egg ladies" in Bismarck. He provided our organically grown poultry as the centerpiece for many festive Thanksgiving and Christmas dinner tables.

Our family enjoyed the magnificent bounty of food provided by our diversified farm. On a freezing January day, our annual beef harvest took place, after which each beef quarter hung wrapped in a thinly worn, discarded clean bed sheet. The beef was aged for ten to fourteen days. Several cutting and wrapping sessions followed. We often made beef sausage, mixed with a small amount of purchased ground pork, using the sausage stuffer Dad's parents had used. Mom also canned beef, a tasty favorite of ours. It served as a fast food at the end of a busy day.

Alongside the protein in the freezer lay a variety of Mom's baked goods, including caramel rolls and various kinds of German *kuchen* (pronounced KOO-ghan). She made six loaves of white bread each week. Sometimes Janine and I were able to talk her into using the dough of the sixth loaf to make German *kechla* (KEYCK-la—the "ck" is the sound of a heavy breath of air, rather than a "c-k" sound)—deep-fried dough that was then dipped into honey or syrup. That was a wonderful, tasty after-school treat!

Mom was not always in favor of deep-frying bread dough. On some bread-baking days, she would succumb to our after-school hunger pleas and let us each consume thick slices of still-warm bread slathered with salted butter. She did not realize that eating one slice of this comfort food would lead to the next and the next and the next until the entire loaf took residence in our tummies. She was aghast!

At Christmastime, Mom always made candy—Peanut Butter Fudge, Speedy Creamy Fudge, and Divinity (pages 260–262). She also baked a variety of cookies—Russian Tea Cakes, Chinese Chews, Seven-Layer Bars, and Oatmeal Crispies (pages 263–267)—and more. Her talented baking skills produced unlimited wintertime treats. Our unheated little front foyer served as a walk-in cooler that provided easy access for sweet-tooth satisfaction!

IT MADE MY MOUTH WATER when observing the bounty of fresh food that the Pfeiffers produced and preserved! Did you experience that, too? The family's excellent supervision over the growth of their crops, garden produce, and livestock rewarded them with filled freezers and larders year after year.

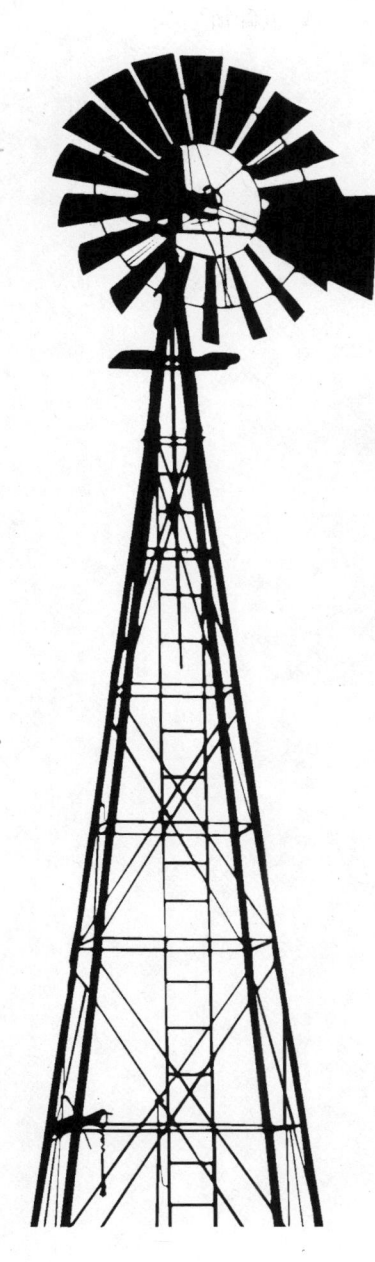

Growing Up Pfeiffer

Chapter 12
The Sisters at Play

IMAGINATIONS—that's what those Pfeiffer girls had! Actually, imaginative play was often typical for kids of the Great Plains during the middle years of the twentieth century. I often caught sight of The Sisters wiling away the daylight hours with make-believe play, assuming adult roles as mothers, bakers, and talented interior and fashion design artists.

Jackie

TELEVISION INFLUENCED much of our imaginary play. Cowboy heroes such as Gene Autry and Roy Rogers relayed the difference between the law-abiding "good guys" and the crooked men. During the summer, we portrayed a variety of moral and corrupt imaginary characters as we galloped around the farmyard on stick-horse steeds.

The farmyard was our work yard and our play yard. In the summertime, Janine and I used Dad's farm shop building, which had been the entry room of the old house, as our playhouse. We'd pack our dolls—Sissy, Betty, and Bonnie—into their buggies and trek across the yard from the house to the shop for an afternoon of play in coolness from the blistering afternoon heat. While the dolls were "napping," we'd create mud pies and cakes, and decorate them with a vast array of farmyard weed seeds using jar lids as pans. (There is a delicate balance of water in proportion to the rich soil to get the perfect texture of a mud pie!) It didn't take our creations long to bake in the hot North Dakota sun!

Indoors, we played "Babbs and Mabbs." Our doll play in the 1950s was influenced by *The Lucille Ball Show*. The location of our make-believe world centered in an apartment building just as Lucy's and Ethel's did. Usually, our real-life bedrooms served as those individual family residences within which Babbs (Jackie) and Mabbs (Janine) were best friends and stay-at-home moms. It was a typical theme and way of life for many women in the 1950s. We pretended that our "husbands," Joe and Mike, were policemen (influenced by the handsome Joe Friday of TV's *Dragnet*) who were steadfast providers for our families. Ideally, when the "boys" came home from work, our babies were on their best behavior, our "apartments" were spic-and-span clean, and supper was on the table!

WHETHER OUR MAKE-BELIEVE house was in our bedrooms or the old shop, inside one of the three wooden boxcars that was destined to be small-grain storage, or in the basement of our home, we girls honed our homemaking skills in preparation for adult years.

Janine

In order to bring hominess to the cement basement wall that served as our "living room" canvas, we young artists used pastel-colored chalks as drawing tools. Our Americana chalk landscape included an outhouse near the farmhouse. The irony within this scene was that our home was one of the few outside the village of Menoken that had running water and a septic tank in the 1950s.

Mom could not seem to share in the artistic gratification that Jackie and I had. She was not the least bit happy when she discovered our chalk drawing on the wall! She didn't make us remove the rustic drawing, though. After we girls became adults and had families of our own, perhaps Mom would reminisce with a few shed tears upon gazing at the creative talent of her then-little girls. The artwork was faded in color but bright in memory!

Jackie

IF WE WEREN'T PLAYING with our soft and cuddly baby dolls, we girls were playing with paper dolls. With body silhouettes constructed of heavy cardstock and clothing designs printed on lighter-weight paper, these dolls were two-dimensional in nature. Did we love to play with paper dolls? Absolutely!

Movie stars of the era—Elizabeth Taylor, Grace Kelly, and Doris Day—were influential favorites of ours. These actresses of the Hollywood silver screen claimed residence within our North Dakota farm home after we traded coins for paper-doll folders at Woolworth's in Bismarck.

Clothing designs for these beautiful celebrities percolated within our minds as our imaginative play with them occupied daylight hours. Their limited paper fashion wardrobes were beautiful but certainly not very vast, to our way of thinking. We spent hours honing our artistic fashion-design talents on lined paper from Big Chief tablets, Crayolas, and well-sharpened colored pencils to create wardrobes worthy of hanging in the closets of starlets!

Janine and I didn't have many toys, but Mom said, "You have enough." And she was probably correct.

INDOOR AND OUTDOOR creative play was alive and well at the Pfeiffers. I expect that you noted that fact, too. When those little girls would play Babbs and Mabbs while clomping around in Eudora's fashionable high heels, each blade of my whirligig was grinning. How thrilled I was to watch their minds at work.

Chapter 13

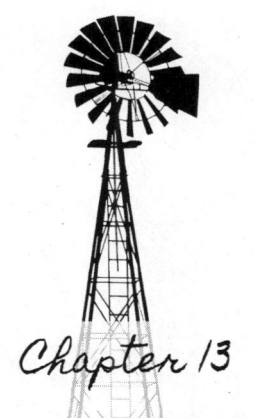

Always Time for Beauty

RURAL WOMEN were talented with needle and thread, both by hand and with sewing machines! They could create the most attractive home-sewn items from the most meager of fabrics—including feed sacks. Quilts, curtains, dresses, aprons, shirts, skirts, pillows, bedspreads—the list was endless. It was as if a rite of passage flowed between old and young when women taught sewing arts to the next generation of seamstresses.

But the "frosting" on the personally presented fashion "cake" was one's hair. Tousled, permed, pin curled, naturally curled, straight-as-a-stick, ponytailed, braided, cut short, blonde, auburn, brunette, black, silver gray, bald as a cue ball. Everyone living on the prairie tended to their chosen hairstyle—if the continually blowing wind allowed.

Above all, God-given beauty was everywhere I gazed on the prairie.

Country Clothing

SEASON TO SEASON, I was appropriately attired in my birthday suit. Neither cotton long underwear, nor four-buckle rubber overshoes, nor flashy one-piece swimsuit covered parts of my strong metal tower for comfort and survival on the prairie.

However, a lack of any wardrobe was impossible for the people of North Dakota! As the thermometer's mercury fluctuated with the changing season, so did the appropriately worn clothing.

The art of fashion design tickled the creative spirits of the Pfeiffer sisters years before they each became accomplished seamstresses. But it was chicken feed—yes, chicken feed—that laid the foundation for fabric selection.

CLOTHING FOR RURAL LIFE was practical—blue jeans, bib overalls for Dad, cotton shirts, sensible shoes, lace-up work shoes, western boots, winter parkas, and front-buckle overshoes.

Insulated coveralls and boots were not available to us in the 1950s. If they had been, doing chores on the frigid, windblown prairie would have been much more comfortable!

I STOOD ON THE EXTREMELY cold iron drawbar of the Farmall M tractor with its attached hay fork as Dad drove it to the hay lot on the west side of the shelterbelt where the cattle and sheep were wintered. It was my job to open the three-strand barbed wire gate and guard the opening so that livestock wouldn't enter the lot as Dad retrieved hay from the stacks.

Janine

My feet were freezing! My legs were chilled to the bone! Long lightweight cotton underwear was worn underneath my jeans, and non-insulated, four-buckle rubber overshoes were worn over my tennis shoes. As I stood moving from one foot to the other, tapping my toes together, I would think, "mind over matter," to try to stay warm. When the cows ate, they excreted steaming plops of manure. At least there was *something of warmth* being produced out there!

My first pair of insulated chore pants was one of the most welcome and most needed Christmas gifts I had ever received as a youngster!

Jackie

OUR APPROPRIATE farm clothing was exchanged for a different mode of dress when our family traveled off the farm to town (Bismarck). Then the bar of attire was raised a few notches. It was especially noticeable in Mom's metamorphosis. She was an accomplished seamstress and had been blessed with a five-foot, eight-inch statuesque figure! When going to town, she would often wear a colorful circular skirt, feminine blouse, and heels, with carefully applied Tangee lipstick as her only nod to facial makeup. This completed the modern summertime look of the 1950s.

We had our own personal dressmaker with Mom! If we needed school clothes, Mom made them, that is, until she had taught sewing skills to us as young 4-Hers. Then we sewed our own. Previous to that time, we had been amateur paper-doll-clothing designers. Our individual imaginations regarding style and design varied. However, we shared a Big Chief tablet of lined paper, and color crayons and pencils to bring our fashionista creativity to life.

Janine

IT WAS OUR rural mailman who played a huge role in our learning about fashion. Two seasons a year, he delivered a marketing masterpiece—a heavy, thickly bound volume known as the mail-order catalog. Sears, Montgomery Ward, Aldens, Spiegel, and J. C. Penney held places of prominence in after-school viewing. A catalog was two inches thick and complete with a "New York runway" of fashions for every member of the family—all at our fingertips!

We didn't need a catalog index to direct us to the pictures, descriptions, and prices of girls' clothing in sizes seven to fourteen. Familiarity with page layout gave license to skip right to the middle of the periodical. Each of us would winnow our selection to our favorite dress, and then Mom would make it for us, but only when it was deemed that a new dress was needed. A new school year, Christmas, and Easter were all times of such need.

Jackie

DURING OUR YOUNG years, flour, chicken laying mash, and baby chick mash/chick starter were purchased in colorfully printed fifty-pound sacks. I did not appreciate having to wear a dress that had once been a chicken feed sack! Imagine shopping at the Peavey Elevator in Bismarck for your next dress or skirt fabric! Little did we know that the farm elevator would serve as our first "fabric store." When Dad instructed us to pick out the mash sacks, we knew we'd end up wearing them!

Janine

KNOWING THAT WE were going to a *real* fabric store to pick out fabric and a pattern was exciting. The basement of J.C. Penney was our usual stop for 4-H clothing-project fabric. We excitedly walked from step to step to the basement landing that brought our young seamstress eyes in direct oneness with hundreds of bolts of fabric.

Mom was extremely patient as she taught us the value of selecting fabric and notions for the pattern style we had chosen. I can only recall one time when she said no to my pattern selection—when the baby-doll look for dresses (similar to baby-doll pajamas) was the current seasonal fad. Mom disapproved of wearing that style in public. I felt so deflated! She openly announced that our hard-earned money from the sale of eggs would not be wasted on a pattern of this design. She added that this seasonal fashion was not necessarily styled for my body shape.

Learning to sew on Mom's treadle Singer sewing machine was a pleasing experience for both Jackie and me. The needle speed was directly determined by the amount of pumping of the foot treadle. Not too fast. Not too slow. This took coordination of hands and feet working together. Stitching an even five-eighths-inch-wide seam allowance was important, and pressing after each sewing step resulted in a more professionally crafted garment. Mom emphasized to us the importance of following these steps.

It was a given that our workmanship would meet our acquired personal standards. This hit home on an oppressively hot, windy summer afternoon when I was sewing a skirt for a 4-H exhibit. The sewing machine resided in Mom and Dad's bedroom. To set the scene for what was to be an uncomfortable situation of sewing, our home had no air conditioning, and I was sewing with wool fabric. I was hot! My physical condition greatly influenced my temperament.

Mom was outside removing clothes from the clothesline. I took my mediocre workmanship to her for inspection. Topstitching of the zipper placket was crooked. I knew full well that her quiet answer would be, "Well, what do you think?" I returned to the sewing machine and had a very heated, one-sided conversation with it as I removed each tiny, inaccurate stitch with the seam ripper!

MOM WAS NOT COLLEGE TRAINED in the craft of sewing. She had learned through experience that "practice makes better."

Jackie

All through our childhood, some garments hanging in our closets had been purchased. I may have had a few ready-made dresses when I was under the age of three, but later pictures of me in a dress always showed me in one made by Mom.

When I was in the second grade, Mom and a few fellow Homemakers Club members attended a National Homemakers Convention in Minneapolis. Upon her return, I was elated when she presented me with a purchased dress in a box labeled Dayton's! The fabric of the dress was a small plaid in royal blue and forest green, with a white lace collar and narrow, black velvet ribbon at the neckline.

Through the years, a few more ready-made dresses hung in my closet. I loved them all immediately! It is not that I didn't appreciate having home-sewn clothes to wear; I just appreciated having purchased clothing like other girls had! My lagging self-esteem prompted me to feel this way. Wearing a commercially constructed dress made me feel as if I fit in with other girls!

Janine

A SPECIAL OCCASION warranted my first purchased dress. As a seven-year-old pianist, I would be competing at the annual North Dakota Federation of Music Clubs contest at Dickinson State Teachers College. Therefore, Mom and I went dress shopping at the Bismarck Sears department store, immediately west of the Northern Pacific Railway depot. The children's clothing was sold on the second floor with fitting rooms facing the railroad tracks. While I tried on a fancy dress with puffed sleeves made of mint-green flocked organza, a rumbling, fast-moving freight train shook the department store like an earthquake on wheels. I was terrified! Nevertheless, Mom made the purchase, and I felt like a princess while wearing the dress!!

READY-MADE OR HOME-SEWN, Jack and Eudora clothed their daughters in appropriate dress no matter what the circumstance dictated. Closets were never lacking in clothing that adapted to the Pfeiffer sisters' maturing changes in clothing sizes. But there was one adorable fashion accessory that was always my favorite. It was the most flattering, too—a smile!

Crowning Glory

THE PFEIFFER SISTERS' crowning glory was their well-coiffed hairstyles, that is, before the North Dakota wind messed them up! Thanks to God the skilled barber, Jack was pretty fortuitous; he didn't have a hairstyle problem!

Janine

IT WAS A SATURDAY afternoon ritual when we were little. One of us pulled a kitchen chair over to the white porcelain double-basin kitchen sink. After we individually ducked our heads underneath the faucet of relaxing, warm running water, Mom placed a small amount of Breck shampoo into the palm of her hand and lathered it into our wet hair. Not many brands of shampoo were available for purchase in the mid-twentieth century. But it would not have mattered in our family. Advertising told us that every lady of any age wanted to be a "pert and pretty Breck girl." We believed it!

Sitting on the wiggly, three-legged stool at the end of the kitchen counter peninsula, I underwent the most trying part of my beauty routine—pin curls. I had not yet developed an attitude of patience for this procedure. By the time the salon session had ended, my

Janine, first grade

head was completely adorned with pin curls created with the help of Mom's left-hand index finger and simple bobby pins. Then I was off to play and let the wind dry my hair. This must have been Mom's go-to hair style, as Jackie had the same coiffure as me. The eventual comb-out was the standard, picture-perfect hairdo for us. Photographs from the 1950s support that.

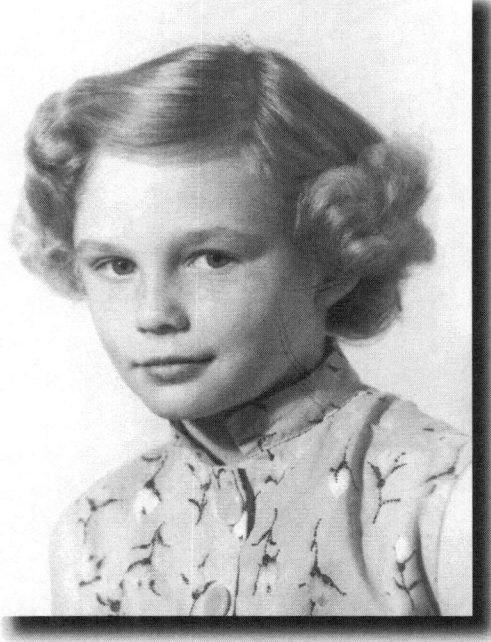

Jackie, fourth grade

Salon styles matured as we sisters did. Eventually, pin curls gave way to brush rollers. Oh, the agony of sleeping with those things on my head! I finally did discover the perfectly contorted body position that let me get a good night's sleep. My, oh my, the suffering we endured in the name of vanity!

When pink sponge rollers became available on the market, Mom latched on to a number of them. They gave the tightest curl and offered the most natural hair-drying comfort. They were a comfortable "win-win" in achieving an eventual curly crowning glory!

However, if Mom wanted me to have curly hair without the need of scheduled time on the kitchen stool, a box of Toni Home Permanent offered everything needed for wash-and-go curl. Words on the box listed "sleek and smooth." A photo showed the same thing. Therefore, I knew that my hair would resemble the photo after going through the process. The permanent solution stunk to high heaven! In addition, the final results of my home perm revealed *nothing* sleek and smooth at all. Frizz—that's what it was! And this result happened each time Mom decided it was time for me to have a perm.

Janine and Jackie exhibiting their curly-wooled 4-H champs while sporting their curly Toni home-permed hair.

Chapter 14

Days We'll Never Forget

LIKE THE FLUCTUATING characteristics of the wind, the days varied! They were traditional. They were unexpected. They brought happiness. They brought fear. Some were out of the ordinary. Some were conventional. Some were casually observed. Some were flamboyantly touted. Some were noted only on the calendar. Some were noted only in one's mind. Some were remarkable. Some did not bear repeating. "Some days were just like that!"

The North Dakota plains harbored a myriad of "some days." I saw them all. People didn't always recognize them.

The Holidays

A WELCOME BREAK—that's what holidays were! Eudora baked special treats. The girls spiffed up the house with the aid of the Electrolux and a swish of the Pledge-sprayed dusting cloth. Jack rose early to take care of the livestock and clear snow from the driveway. Whoosh! There he went, driving the Farmall M tractor with its attached loader bucket collecting snow from the previous night's generous precipitous deposit.

It was a time to join grandpa, grandma, aunts, uncles, and cousins. Our place or theirs. Winter or summer. Clear skies or pelting snow. It was time to gather and break bread together.

Janine WEBSTER'S DICTIONARY defines a holiday as a day of festivity or recreation when no work is done. That might be true in many families, but for livestock families such as ours, even on those special days we dedicated a few hours to the care of livestock both morning and evening, with holiday festivities sandwiched in between.

Holidays are often the source of family gatherings and of rituals. These get-togethers reinforce values and beliefs, and contribute to a sense of belonging. Our family did not observe every calendar holiday with relatives. Yet what stands out are three special "relative" occasions.

Decoration Day, as Memorial Day was called before 1967, was a time when we reconnected with our maternal legacy at Oakes. We spent the morning placing flowers beside the gravestones of family who had gone before us. Respect for the deceased was observed by carefully walking around the grave and never on top of or across it. We still follow that same cemetery etiquette as adults. This solemnity was followed by a picnic and cousin fun in the cool shade of the orchard on Grandma and Grandpa Wiese's farm.

Oh-so-many Thanksgivings ago, in country school on the North Dakota prairie, our teacher, Mrs. Arntz, sat at the well-tuned, upright piano and taught us the words to *Over the River and Through the Woods*.

As a first-grader, I knew that seasonal song had been written especially for me! Here is the reason why: Mom's family lived a distance from us at Oakes, North Dakota. Even though an often-occurring Thanksgiving Day blizzard blew fiercely through the upper Great Plains, our family arose in the dark, frigid early morning hours for the over-the-river-and-through-the-woods excursion.

Dad had arisen even earlier to feed our cattle and sheep with a double amount of hay from haystacks he had created in the blazing summertime heat with pitchfork and Farmhand hay bucker. He knew full well that our return destination in the nighttime hours would be way past the livestock's normal feeding time. As the conscientious animal husbandman that he was, our livestock never lacked for food or attention.

Dad had made certain that the car had been filled with gas and warmed up, ready for the family to embark. The backseat window of our 1957 two-tone green Buick sedan was the designated safe place for Mom's beautifully created pumpkin and apple pies, and light-as-a-feather yeast rolls. Armed with winter traveling clothing and blankets, our family over-the-river motored to see our grandma, aunts, uncles, and cousins.

As many a child riding for a long distance has been known to have impatiently questioned, "Are we there yet?" was the repetitious inquiry of Jackie and me during the two-and-a-half-hour trip. Finally, we arrived at Grandma Wiese's house near Oakes for a brief, joyous reunion with her. (Grandpa had died in 1957 after a fall from the barn roof.) Our stay there was momentary because our good-natured, petite grandma joined us in the "sleigh." Then the "horse [that] knew the way" continued to its South Dakota destination of Arrowhead Ranch, Hecla. Soon, we stopped next to the ranch house of my aunt and uncle, Merna and Harold Treeby.

We are a very huggy family, so it took a few minutes for every adult and child to be made welcome with a smile and enthusiastic embrace.

UPON ARRIVAL I ENTERED the kitchen and noticed that the big sink held a mound of potatoes. Little did I know that I was about to have an intimate relationship with that pile of spuds!

Jackie

The moms and we two oldest cousins—Colin Treeby and me—helped prepare the food for the family feast. Before we could head outside to mess around with the horses, Aunt Merna informed us that those potatoes needed to be peeled! I calmly complied and began peeling, carefully moving the peeler toward me as I'd been taught. Colin grumbled and slowly made his way to the sink. That's where his sluggishness ended! When he started the task, it was evident this was not the first time he'd performed this chore! He whipped off four slices to my one, moving the peeler in rapid succession, flicking the peelings toward the far side of the sink. I paused, looked in awe at his method, and began to copy it. Thanks to his lesson in "how to peel potatoes efficiently," we were able to head outside more quickly. Even today, I continue to use the Colin method of peeling potatoes as I think of him when delving into this task.

Janine

AFTER A VERY FILLING noon meal with roasted turkey and all of the trimmings, we cousins ventured out into freezing temperatures for an afternoon game of tag. This was not the normal game of tag; it was tag played on horseback! After the horses were saddled, we cousins rode away to the hay lot where haystacks had been placed earlier in the year as winter cattle feed. Tall, wind-blown snowbanks made it difficult for our mounts to zigzag around the haystacks in order to outrun the team of person and horse who was "it." What great fun that was!

As the sun began to set in the west, there were no snowflakes visible. The Buick's motor was started, and we were homeward bound. One year, however, before we saw the mailbox at the end of our driveway, we had driven in a raging blizzard on US Highway 10. Jackie and I sat huddled together under warm, woolen blankets in order to share body heat. Dad managed to keep the heavy car on the highway while Mom served as the navigator. She stuck her scarf-covered head out of the open passenger-side window into the pelting snow in order to have a bird's-eye view of the painted line that separated the driving lane from the road's shoulder and ditch.

Mom called to Dad, "You're doing fine. Just keep going!" This definitely was a lesson in operator patience, as Dad's driving speed during normal winter driving conditions was consistently over the speed limit! Our car never wandered off the pavement into the snow-filled ditch. Thank goodness! When the North Dakota Department of Transportation repainted those highway lines in the summertime, Mom often commented, "Why do they paint those lines white instead of yellow? How can we ever see white lines in a blizzard?" Right, she was!

Reflecting on our Thanksgiving gatherings, why did we ever risk our lives traveling in the north country's winter elements? Strangely, year after year, we were more likely to have a blizzard on that day than not. The answer to my question is twofold: we lived daily in that environment and knew how to work within the dangers it could deliver; and Dad knew that if there was any way possible that Mom could revel in the physical presence of her mom, siblings, nieces, and nephews, she could "refuel" until she saw them again in another six months. It was Dad's love gift to his "Dode."

WHEN LIVING IN North Dakota in the mid-twentieth century, Christmas without snow on the ground—and lots of it—was rare. With the frigid, ubiquitous wind that blew south out of Canada, fighting drifted snow on highways and byways was the Christmas "present" we tried to avoid unwrapping. The weather, along with Mom and Dad's desire to create our own family's fond Christmas memories, were the catalysts to stay home.

Our annual Christmas card list found its way out of hibernation the beginning of each December. Selling boxed Christmas cards was an every-year money-making

Jackie and Janine trimming the tree, 1955.

project offered by the Menoken Homemakers Club. Mom purchased her fair share of those beautiful cards as Merry Christmas greetings were sent to dozens of family and friends. A handwritten family epistle was included with the greetings sent to those who lived far away.

I often helped Mom with this task by licking the postage stamps and affixing one to the upper right-hand corner of each envelope. With just a few copper pennies, one could buy a postage stamp. However, every envelope did not require the same amount of postage. If the envelope was sealed shut, a three-cent stamp was adhered to the envelope. If gently tucking the envelope's flap inside the opening was the method used for privacy, only a two-cent stamp was applied. At our house, only cards that contained a personal letter within the folds of the card were sealed with my saliva. Had we sent a postcard instead of a letter, the cost would have only been a pretty penny. Mom always felt charitable and purchased colorful Christmas seals from Boys Town in Nebraska and the Crippled Children's Home in Jamestown.

Excitedly, Jackie and I were co-chairmen of the annual house decoration committee. Our fresh Christmas tree was dressed with glass balls; papier-mâché bells; strings of large, colorful lights; miniature glass-ball garland, and thin tinsel icicles. Virtuous patience was practiced with the placement of each individual silver strand. It was a Christmas-decorating sin to throw those shimmering strands onto a bough!

After the new year had begun, returning all of the decorations to their storage boxes was an emotional letdown. In addition, each of those silver strands needed to be just as carefully removed from the tree as they had been applied, in order to reuse them for the next year. Exasperation!

NORTH DAKOTA entrepreneur Harold Schafer had introduced his newly created product Glass Wax in 1945. Mom used this to clean the windows of our new home. It was more than a glass cleaner, though. After the pink liquid was poured into a little bowl, Glass Wax Christmas Stencils were pressed on to the living room picture window and large wall mirror by our little hands. With the aid of a sponge, we applied Glass Wax to the paper stencils with several little taps. The dried pink liquid morphed into the appearance of white snow. Christmas trees, Santa's sleigh and reindeer, a nativity scene, the words Merry Christmas, and other designs added to the atmosphere.

We were almost set for Santa's arrival! The last task was to put out cookies and milk for the jolly man and carrots for Rudolph and his peers.

BREAKFAST WAS SPECIAL! It wasn't every day that we got to eat our Christmas tree! Nor did we have slices of fresh, intensely flavored, juicy oranges for eating enjoyment on days other than Christmas. They were too expensive! Now then, what was this Christmas tree that we consumed?

As little girls, Mom often made her fluffy cinnamon rolls on Christmas Eve day. Rather than place each pinwheel slice of dough stuffed with cinnamon and brown sugar into a nine-by-thirteen-inch baking pan, she placed those spirals in the shape of a Christmas tree on her shiny aluminum cookie sheets. A color palette of Christmas sugar sprinkles and silver dragées was then artistically given residence on the tree shape by us Sisters. It was a baking masterpiece and truly a tasty Christmas tradition!

It wouldn't have been Christmas without the

> *Year after year, Christmas morning was celebrated in this order: get out of bed, eat breakfast, feed the livestock, and then open presents. Even as adults with young children whose family's livelihood depended on livestock, we've annually practiced the same December 25th morning routine.*
>
> *Janine*

heartwarming fun of making decorated rolled sugar cookies of many traditional shapes. Aluminum cookie cutters were tucked away on the lower shelf of Mom's baking cupboard awaiting their once-a-year appearance. Mom gave us carte blanche when it came time to decorate them. If we made a mess while doing this craft, Mom never complained. She allowed us to explore the science and art of baking with patience and encouragement, knowing full well that "practice makes better."

Those Christmas baking traditions made a lasting pleasurable imprint that stayed with us as we moved into our own homes after marriage and children.

Janine

UNWRAPPING COLORFUL red and green curling ribbon that had been "zipped" over a scissor's blade into ringlets on the tops of festively wrapped boxes brought gifts of needs and gifts of wants. It was a fact that during a certain period of my life, I would get a new white nylon full slip even if I thought I didn't need it. I have always had a knack for guessing the contents of a wrapped package. Therefore, when the flat eight-and-a-half-by-eleven-inch box with my name on it peeked out from underneath our gaily lighted tree, I thought to myself, "Oh, no. Not another slip!" Sure enough, there it was, reposing within the folds of crinkly, white tissue paper in all its pristinely white tricot and lace splendor!

However, there were some special gifts for us that drew squeals of excitement! One year, the gift tag on a huge box was addressed to me. Inside were two dolls. I christened them Janine and Charlene. They looked identical except Charlene was twice the size. They didn't walk or wet as some dolls of that era did, but I loved them for many years. A wicker doll buggy, a beautiful little carriage, snugly transported them hither and yon all around the farmyard.

THERE WERE ALWAYS enough packages under the tree for which we were thankful. Yet in 1957, Dad seriously said to me, "Come sit down here. Mom and I need to tell you something." I thought, "Oh my! What's wrong?" Fear touched me! As we three sat at the kitchen table, Dad relayed that it had been a poor crop year. That meant there was little money for extras, including a number of Christmas presents. The news was distressing to me. I had never felt that our family was financially poor until I heard this message. I began to worry about what that might mean in my life as a ten-year-old. However, I felt gratifying pride that Mom and Dad would include me in this adult situation.

AS CALENDAR PAGES CHANGED, I saw cherished traditions evolve during family gatherings that connected and expanded relationships. These special times helped to foster a sense of security and identity for The Sisters.

An Unexpected Visitor

I RECALL THE TIME the girls were calmly playing with their paper dolls when what could have been tragic destruction to the family was averted. After that deafening boom, my ears were disturbingly affected and strained to hear the sweet sounds of the prairie.

Jackie

ONE EARLY SUMMER afternoon in June 1954 our paper-doll fantasy world turned into tumultuous reality! Shortly after dinner, we sisters were sitting on Janine's double bed playing paper dolls. The blue sky featured fluffy, white cumulus clouds. I remember looking out the south-facing window having two observations: an unusually large cloud, large enough to block out the sun, had just passed, and the airplane I spotted in a split-second view was flying way too low! I quickly put two and two together, and realized that the darkening cloud had really been the shadow of the airplane!

Within about fifteen seconds a terrifying loud boom shook the house! The plane had crashed into our corn field after having barely cleared the tops of the evergreens of the shelterbelt west of our house.

As was Dad's habit after eating the noon meal, he had been rejuvenating himself with a quick fifteen-minute nap while lying on the cool kitchen floor. The shock of this booming explosive sound abruptly awakened him and caused tremendous confusion. Dad shot out of the house toward the garage! In his temporarily confused state of mind, he threw open one of the heavy doors located behind the parked car, then quickly slammed it closed when nothing seemed amiss. In continued confusion, he opened the second door and scurried on to the Farmall M tractor and headed for the plume of black smoke that was spouting from the earth.

In the chaos, Mom sprinted after him! As I was running after her, she shouted to me, "Stay there, and take care of your sister." At age seven, I was in no emotional shape to do that. I was scared! I ran after her, and Janine ran after me, sobbing, "Wait for me!" I can remember feeling a little guilty for not stopping for her. However, I was in self-preservation mode, and I was so frightened! I wanted the safety of my mom. Of course, Janine was frightened also, her tears of fright mixed with the dust of the field road.

Janine: YOU MIGHT WONDER why there was dust in the air. A parade of cars containing concerned onlookers was moving to the crash site through our farmyard past us toward the mushrooming black smoke rising from the earth. I recall thinking that I was going to get run over if the drivers couldn't see me running through the billowing dust that rose from their spinning tires!

Jackie: IN RETROSPECT, the scene in the field looked as if it were a devastating volcanic eruption. From a June 12, 1954, news article in *The Bismarck Tribune,* we later learned that the pilot had parachuted from the F-86D jet fighter about six-and-a-half miles above the earth. The flight had originated at Ellsworth Air Force Base near Rapid City, South Dakota.

The pilot had safely landed about ten miles to the east of our farm near McKenzie. A passing motorist helped him collapse his parachute and then drove him to the Bismarck airport. Meanwhile, the unmanned plane flew itself into our corn field!

Bismarck Tribune – June 12, 1954

'Chutes 6 ½ M to Earth

An F-86D jet fighter from Ellsworth Air Force Base at Rapid City crashed and exploded in a field near Menoken, ten miles east of Bismarck, shortly after noon Saturday.

Pilot of the aircraft, 2nd Lt. Arnold Weber, Eldorado, Kan., bailed out of the aircraft nearly seven miles up and parachuted to safety east of McKenzie, some ten miles away.

Weber, who was uninjured, was assisted in his landing by a passing motorist, Joseph Swartz, Bismarck. Swartz helped the pilot collapse his parachute and then drove him to the Bismarck airport.

Meanwhile authorities were combing the area where the plane crashed, reportedly looking for secret equipment supposed to have been aboard the plane. A tight security guard was thrown around the crash area.

Weber was on a routine training flight with one other jet when he heard an explosion in the rear of his plane.

"I didn't know what it was," he told a Bismarck Tribune reporter at the airport, where he was calling Rapid City to report the crash.

"My wing man radioed from his plane, 'Son, you've got something. I don't know what. You'd better get out.'"

"I tried to pull back on the throttle," Weber continued, "but nothing happened, so I pushed the ejector button."

He was catapulted into the atmosphere, 35,000 feet above the earth.

"I knew that if I'd tried to breathe, I would black out," the youthful appearing pilot said, "so I held my breath as long as I could. I must have opened the chute at around 15,000 feet."

Weber did not know how long it took him to float to the ground. "It seemed like half an hour," he said, half jokingly.

"I knew that it was going to

(continued pg. 216)

An armed Air Force security guard had been placed at the driveway to our farmstead, and a security detail was also stationed around the crash site. The excitement lasted for about a week.

Besides the never-to-be-forgotten memories, tangible items continued to remind us of the event. For years and years afterward, Dad turned up chartreuse-green/silver plane parts while working the soil. The earth itself was permanently fractured, for even today a dip in the earth can be seen where the jet had crashed.

For us frightened-to-death little girls, the happy memory of playing paper dolls was darkened by the airplane accident that bright, mid-day Saturday.

'Chutes 6 ½ M to Earth

be a jolt when I opened that 'chute, so I braced myself for it. You'd be surprised at the things you think about at a time like that."

Weber recalled that he fell through the sky "every which way."

"I wanted to see the ground when I was falling," he said, "so I put one arm to turn me over. I'd flip over on my stomach, but as soon as I'd bring my arm back in, I'd slip back on my back."

"When I hit," Weber stated, "I couldn't spill the wind out of my 'chute and it dragged me 100 yards. If that other fellow (Swartz) hadn't come up when he did I think I'd still be in it."

Weber has been in the Air Force for 2½ years. He is married and has no children. He weighs about 200 pounds and stands 6 feet, 2 inches tall. Ellsworth AFB officials told Weber they would send a C-47 plane to Bismarck to pick him up and return him to Rapid City later in the afternoon.

Swartz is an employee of the Sun Oil Co. here.

IMAGINE YOURSELF in this situation: the routine schedule of an innocent, bright summer day turned to chaotic confusion. That was the terrifying backdrop for Jack, Eudora, and the girls. Fear of the unknown clung to the coattails of the Pfeiffer family. The calamity of the day eventually turned to peaceful calm—memories forever embedded within the fabric of the mind.

What Was So Special about Friday?

JUST LIKE CLOCKWORK, when Friday rolled around, the car was packed with cases and cartons of fresh-from-the-farm eggs—dozens of them! Along with the eggs, when Jack was still able to milk cows, milk cans were loaded into the trunk's expanse. Every Friday was "egg day," or "town day"— the Pfeiffers' weekly trading trip to Bismarck.

The egg-delivering ritual transpired on Fridays, but it took the previous six days of dedicated work by well-tended laying hens, along with Jackie and Janine's egg-gathering skills and Eudora's clean presentation of those eggs, to help bring "egg day" to fruition.

As the car zoomed out of the graveled driveway, I could see that this trip to Bismarck included more than an accumulation of cash for the eggs to be sold. On Fridays during school vacations when the four Pfeiffers took this weekly trip to Bismarck, an exhibition of life skills and family oneness occurred from the time the car left home until I watched its return.

Jackie

AS WE MOTORED into Bismarck from the east on US Highway 10, our sensitive young noses were assaulted by the pungent, unforgettable aroma of sharp, acrid yeast from the ovens of the Sweetheart Bakery on East Main Street. It was such a contrast from the comforting balm produced by smaller bakeries and by Mom's oven during her weekly bread-baking session.

In the early 1950s, Schultz Creamery was our first Friday-morning stop in Bismarck—as long as Dad was still milking cows. The large car trunk had been meticulously packed with produce from our farm—cases of eggs and tightly covered, ten-gallon metal milk cans.

A distinctly damp environment met us as we entered the creamery. Behind the glass windows of the sales room, floors were continually showered with water to keep the processing room clean and sanitary.

The creamery rented frozen-food locker space, which served as a small, out-of-home freezer. The lockers appeared to be similar to modern-day gym lockers. However, they were made of sturdy wire to allow air flow around the frozen food. The face of each locker was a hinged door that was numbered and sealed by a keyed padlock. This service was offered to the general public for a nominal rental fee.

We sisters accompanied Dad into that giant compartmentalized walk-in freezer whose walls were heavily laden with thick frost and ice. It was freezing cold behind those heavy twelve-inch-thick doors. I was glad that Dad knew the route to our rented space, as it seemed as though we trudged in a zigzagging maze in order to reach the space that held our packages of beef. As Dad unlocked the door to our unit and retrieved the frozen brick-like packages, Janine and I entertained ourselves by blowing out air in order to see our breath. I always felt safe in there with Dad, but my reasoning told me that I would not be able to open those doors by myself!

Our early-morning stop at the creamery helped reduce the vehicle's produce load, but it was the late-afternoon retrieval of empty milk cans that Janine and I anticipated. Dad often spent a tiny portion of his milk check for a Popsicle or ice cream bar for his girls.

Janine

AS OUR FAMILY worked and relaxed together on Fridays, I did not have a smidgen of realization that those occurrences would serve as the building blocks for my future. In retrospect, they played a gigantic role in forging my personal growth and my destiny!

After unloading the cans from the trunk, we began our morning egg route, always stopping first at the home of the Wehri family. Dad was a natural-born peddler and delivered our farm-fresh eggs to all strata of society. Even North Dakota Governor John Davis enjoyed eggs laid by our chickens. Dad and he had been boyhood friends on the prairie. Then their lives meandered in different directions in their teen and young adult years. One chose the path of speaking for the people. The other chose to feed the people. Be that as it may, they became reunited due to one common denominator—our farm-fresh eggs.

Jackie and I observed Dad's personal attention to genuine customer service. He was an honest businessman! He delighted in having us accompany him as he sold eggs in the city's professional offices. Carefully nestled within our little-girl arms, Jackie and I proudly carried string-wrapped cartons of two or three dozen eggs as Dad happily carried a durable cardboard case of fifteen dozen eggs. Dad was in his realm; if he could have cheerfully whistled while he carted that egg case around, he would have! His false teeth prevented that musical sound from his pursed lips.

We rode the elevators of those buildings, delivering eggs to executives and their secretaries. How exciting it was for us farm girls to push the elevator buttons for the designated floors! We took note of Dad's mental math skills as he made change from the pockets of his clean navy-blue-and-white-striped overalls. A genuine smile and a polite "thank you" were always extended to those who bought our product. He never grew tired of conversing. Our egg customers loved buying from Dad; he delivered a quality product along with outstanding camaraderie. One couldn't help but want to do business with Jack Pfeiffer!

On "egg day," we always took our noon meal at Grandpa and Grandma Pfeiffer's house on North Eleventh Street. Our Germans from Russia heritage was apparent in Grandma's expertise in gently stretching strudel dough until it was as "thin as underpants" (an expression we girls had coined)! Grandma's practiced hands had the knack of stretching the dough so thinly that it was translucent, much like the thin material of our "dainties." Then she'd cut the dough into strips, roll into ropes, let rest, cook it in boiling water, and serve it with melt-in-your-mouth roast beef, boiled potatoes, and gravy. This strudel is not a dessert. If only I could enjoy that gastronomical treat today!

Mom usually had accumulated a generous shopping list over a week's time. In the afternoon, we girls accompanied her as she made purchases at a variety of businesses in downtown Bismarck where she wisely taught the practice of sage money management to Jackie and me. "Money doesn't grow on trees, girls," she would tell us. As a rule, our parents practiced thrifty spending, but they often spent a few coins on sweets. Dad loved sweets. Actually, he loved to eat most anything. Among those traits I inherited from Dad, my enjoyment of food is one of them!

When stepping inside the local Osco Drug, we were greeted by an island-shaped candy counter. Dad made the candy selections that would accompany us out the door. In the mid-twentieth century, candy bars cost five cents and ten cents. All candy bars appeared to be the same size to my young eyes. Therefore, I have no explanation as to why the price was double for those that caught the attention of my yearning. Perhaps the ingredients contained within my hopeful choices were more costly than those in the five-cent kinds. Even though I yearned for a Rolo bar or a maple-flavored Nut Goodie, they each cost ten cents. "A penny saved is a penny earned," as Mom would often quote.

AFTER OUR SHOPPING journey was completed and Dad's egg route was concluded, we rendezvoused at Finney Drug on the corner of Fourth Street and Broadway where a refreshing Buffalo Nut Sundae (similar to what is known today as a Tin Roof Sundae), served invitingly in a sparkling parfait glass, awaited us after ordering. I can still visualize the ice cream treat's preparation—beginning at the bottom of the glass: one pump of rich chocolate syrup, one round scoop of vanilla ice cream, second pump of rich chocolate syrup, second round scoop of vanilla ice cream, spoonful of sticky pure-white marshmallow crème, and a healthy sprinkle of chopped salted peanuts. Divine! We became weekly friends with the two regular soda jerks—the solemn, slim, gray-bunned "malted milk lady" and the more talkative "ice cream lady" who Jackie and I referred to as "Grandma."

Mom and Dad expected us girls to exhibit polite manners in public. Therefore, we refrained from spinning on the red Naugahyde seats of the soda fountain stools. Being polite was such a drag sometimes! As we sat on the motionless stools and saw our reflections in the full-width mirror behind the soda fountain, we felt serenely blanketed in love to be with our family for a Friday afternoon treat.

Jackie

ONE FRIDAY, AS OUR FAMILY walked out of Finney's after enjoying our afternoon sweet treat, I noticed the omnipresent old man with the broom. He was a tall, gray-bearded vagabond and was often seen walking the downtown streets. No matter what the season, it appeared that his long, dark wool coat and long-handled push broom were continually part of his persona. We assumed he was without a home. When we met him face-to-face on the street, I noticed that he seemed to have kind blue eyes. His cadence was slowly purposeful. His demeanor was one of loneliness. After passing him on the sidewalk, Mom gently shared, "Always be kind to old people. One day, you, too, will be old." I've never forgotten that.

Janine ANOTHER AFFECTIONATE memory is associated with Finney Drug—a certain gift purchased there that was Dad's love gift to Mom. Written record does not include the full story, and memory is dim as to our parents' conversations about their early dating years. Even then, spending money on frivolous items was very rare! Nevertheless, a beautiful lipstick-pink-colored tin of candy known as Almond Roca was purchased annually by Dad from Finney Drug. It was his love gift to Mom. No gift wrap needed. No pretty bow added. Just an eye-catching container. Each time Dad was the bearer of this special almond-coated butter crunch toffee, Mom smiled with delight and lovingly chided, "Oh, Jack!" Savoring the sweet treat was a delight. And watching Dad kiss Mom as he gave her the gift was and still is a memorable occasion in our parents' love story!

Finney Drug is full of time-lapse recollections for me. It sported a mechanical pinto horse. What child didn't yearn to ride a pony like that—especially one that didn't buck? I longed for Mom to offer a silver nickel, enabling me to sit astride the horse's black leather saddle and gently lope in rocking-chair comfort! As she solemnly denied my request, she stated, "Why do you want to ride that horse when you have a real horse at home?" Mom spoke words of truth. But the thing she was forgetting was that this horse did not buck when I rode it as my Shetland pony, Ginger, did!

The activities at Finney Drug were satisfying, but the "frosting" on my Friday cake was our trip to the grocery store. I still treasure those supermarket shopping experiences, and even today, one of my favorite places to shop is the grocery store. As a professional baker, when my eyes scan a plethora of various ingredients stocked on the shelves, I envision creating new recipes with unlimited baking possibilities.

Mom let Jackie and me take turns perching on the front of the cart as she pushed it from aisle to aisle. But the times I had the opportunity to push my own little, shiny, junior-sized cart alongside her were when I felt so grown up!

The grocery store cash register was a magnet to me. Women checkers operated the tills as if they themselves were well-oiled machines—manually pushing the numerically labeled buttons here and there, and then punching the larger rectangular knob with the right side of their fists. "Cha-ching," the machine would ring as the price of the product was recorded within its inner workings. Some little girls wanted to grow up to be a nurse or a teacher. I wanted to be a grocery checker—knowledgeable, fast, efficient, and all with a friendly smile for the customer!

Free S&H Green Stamps were given in thanks for trading at Red Owl. The more hard-earned dollars we spent for groceries, the more stamps we received. After returning home from town, Jackie or I hastily licked that awful-tasting glue on the backs of the stamps and pasted them into designated stamp books. When we had accumulated enough filled books of stamps, they were redeemed for "free" items such as a card table and chairs and croquet set at the redemption center in Bismarck. Our family enjoyed a host of these "freebies."

All in all, Friday events with my family taught me many lessons: the value of a dollar; the importance of treating a person fairly; the financial outcome of responsible caretaking of an investment; growth in the bond of our family as we worked and played together; and, of course, the wonderland of a grocery store!

THAT DAY—FRIDAY. FOR THE PFEIFFERS, I believe it was distinctly the time when the roots of family life meandered deeper into the sisters' characters. Whether or not Jackie and Janine knew it at the time, the activities of a Friday were instrumental in developing wings to soar beyond their nest of home.

Chapter 15
Lessons in Life and Art

A GAMUT OF FACTORS influenced the pace of life on the prairie.

Work! Work! Work! It was the key to survival.

Yet participation in the fine arts brought a breath of fresh air from the ordinary heartbeat of activity. The poetry of life was in motion as realism became romance, skill became grace, and melody became harmony.

An education outside the confines of a four-sided school building exhibited unobtrusive instruction in family values that were imprinted on each generation. Youngsters learned simple acts of kindness, common courtesies, and the value of a dollar from the everyday teachings of their parents and grandparents. They were "cutting their teeth" on the broad land of the Great Plains.

Practicing Our Talents

LIFE ON THE FARM within the Menoken community was the centerpiece of the Pfeiffers' existence. But in their parental wisdom, Jack and Eudora offered their daughters opportunities beyond the farm that helped prepare them for their individual solo "flights."

Jackie

JANINE AND I were very fortunate that Mom and Dad valued education! Attending college after high school had always been an unspoken family expectation. Our parents realized that there was much more to learn beyond the schoolhouse walls. Consequently, we were given the opportunity to have a variety of lessons in the ten-miles-away capital city of Bismarck.

We will always be grateful that Mom and Dad knew there was value in learning to read music. For our family, that meant learning to play the piano. Mom, who played from pieces of sheet music and hymnals, had been taught to play by her mother. Dad had played the clarinet in the Goodrich High School band. Dad's clarinet now resides in the home of his great-granddaughter who is a middle-school clarinetist.

Jackie, age eleven

As an adult, I came to appreciate those years of piano lessons. I was told that I had what was termed a "good touch." The often-forgotten byproduct of learning to play an instrument is the gift of learning to read music. That capability has been paramount in enhancing my ability in choral singing, as well as playing the dulcimer, ukulele, Omnichord, and handbells.

At just the right time, we inherited our paternal grandma's upright grand piano. It had been given to her on her seventeenth birthday by her father, Jakob Brost, who owned a mercantile in their small North Dakota prairie town, Goodrich. My daughters used the piano for their piano education, and it will be passed on to the next generation.

Taking piano lessons was fine with me, but I really wanted to take dance lessons! Finally, Mom agreed, which meant I'd have piano and dance lessons each week. I started both lessons while in the third grade. Being at Connie's Dance Studio

Jackie, first-grade Christmas operetta

in Bismarck on Thursdays after school was the highlight of my week! Through the years, I learned ballet, tap, and pointe.

My teacher, Connie Kuntz, was from Austria, and the numbered tattoo on her arm was my first introduction to one of the many atrocities of World War II. She was married to a North Dakota/American soldier, Lee Kuntz, in Vienna in 1947, and they came to Bismarck in 1949.

Every year Mrs. Kuntz's studio held a dance recital at the Bismarck Auditorium. The building had greeted its first audience in January 1914. It was fun for me to dance in this old theatre! I felt a kinship with the bygone dancers' and actors' spirits that loomed in this building.

Beneath the stage's scuffed, hardwood floor lay a basement and sub-basement filled with long narrow halls lit with caged, single light bulbs intermittently spaced; dressing rooms with rows of bright lights above the full-length, walled mirrors; and the still-clinging aromas of sweaty bodies of forgotten performers. When the heavy, maroon velvet stage curtains opened to a packed house, the entire environment felt exhilarating. I loved being a part of the theatre!

Even though I loved dancing, I took lessons for only three years. A combination of being embarrassed by my blossoming body, which a tight leotard revealed, and more involvement in 4-H caused me to put my dancing on hold for many years. But I did return to the stage, again and again!

I inherited my love of dance from Mom. One of my early memories is of Mom holding me as she sang while we waltzed around the house. She loved to dance! Perhaps Mom was willing to drive me to dance lessons because it had been something that she had wanted to do as a child, but the opportunity had not been available.

Janine

MONEY WAS NOT in generous supply for extras. I started piano lessons at age five, and after studying thirteen years with the best, most highly acclaimed piano teacher, Belle Mehus, I came to realize how Dad and Mom must have truly sacrificed financially in order for those lessons to occur. Miss Mehus had received accolades for her dedicated teaching talents from her students and professional peers throughout the United States. The charge was $3 for a half-hour lesson. This was a vast expense for a North Dakota small-farm family in the 1950s and '60s. Not only that, but it meant extra trips to town, which added up to more dollars spent for the car's gas for the pursuit of the arts in our family.

With my developing piano talent and dedication, Miss Mehus featured my abilities in a classical solo piano recital. I cannot tell you why, but it was very important to her that I present this recital before my eleventh birthday. The date set was Sunday, June 24, 1961, seven days prior to that birthday.

At the Wylie Piano Company in Bismarck, in preparation for my recital all of the pianos were moved to the side of the room, and chairs were set up for the intended audience. Mom made a beautiful yellow sleeveless dress from embroidered pima cotton fabric for me to wear for the event. I felt like a princess! It continued to be one of my favorite dresses to wear while I was still that size. *Knight Rupert* by Robert Schumann is the only song

Janine at her piano recital, 1961

I remember from that half-hour recital. I can still play parts of it! In retrospect, it is noteworthy that June 24, 1961, was also the eleventh birthday of my husband.

Miss Mehus and I grew to have a loving relationship with each other. I do not recall ever exchanging a hug; she didn't express her feelings in that manner. However, her twinkling eyes and broad smile related warmth. She was quite demanding concerning the shape of my hands and the length of my fingernails while playing. Until the correct hand pose was ingrained into my muscle memory, her hand would gently cover and shape my hand to the correct piano-playing posture. If her ears noticed the clicking of fingernails hitting the keyboard while I was playing, she immediately retrieved a small cuticle scissors and shortened my nails.

With the piano foundation set, I became Belle Mehus's "student with promise." She groomed me to accompany the highly acclaimed Bismarck High School Symphony Orchestra under the direction of Harold Van Heuvelen. Then, as an eleventh-grader, I was the featured piano soloist performing Beethoven's Piano Concerto No. 2 in B Flat Major, Opus 19 with the Orchestra. With a glowing heart, my Grandma Pfeiffer often told me, "My buttons are busting!" She and Grandpa were part of an enthusiastic audience in Bismarck's spacious World War Memorial Building for the event.

Jackie

THE SUMMER BEFORE my fifth-grade year, the neighborhood mothers decided to organize a carpool to Bismarck for swimming lessons. I was the oldest child of the group and embarrassed to be in the beginning class with the little kids. However, I progressed and passed the beginning and intermediate tests. Jumping off the low diving board was fine, but I was not comfortable jumping off the high dive! Nonetheless, I needed to do that to pass one of the tests, and it took me a while to work up the courage to do it. I accomplished proficiency at the several mandatory strokes and at treading water for three minutes. Swimming is certainly not my first choice of physical activity, but I'm glad to have the skill.

The lessons were held at the Elks Swimming Pool on the west side of the city. Bismarck's first Dairy Queen was conveniently located across the street from the pool. Janine and I were always given a dime so that we could buy a treat after the lessons. My usual choice was a Dilly Bar. If you were lucky at the end of consuming your treat, you'd see the word *free* stamped on the wooden, tongue depressor-size stick. Unfortunately for me, that word didn't appear very often.

The summer before my seventh grade year our neighbor, Millie McCormick, who was a registered nurse working at Bismarck's St. Alexius Hospital, formed a baton twirling class. She was a really big lady in body and soul and voice! The words *jolly* and *hearty laugh* were associated with her. She was a joyous sight to behold as she twirled and pranced; her entire body moved with the music! And man, could she control that baton!

The twirling class performed to a variety of peppy marches, such as John Philip Sousa's *The Stars and Stripes Forever*. Music blared from a record player as its pinpoint needle traveled the groove on the 78-rpm vinyl record.

Our performance costumes were comprised of white Keds shoes, starched white cotton blouses, and crisp navy-blue shorts. How were those fabric shoes kept spotlessly white? By using a little dabber to apply white liquid shoe polish, which often leaked through the fabric, resulting in white feet!

Learning from Example

TABLE ETIQUETTE was learned from the example of our parents, grandparents, and teachers. We practiced proper table manners at home and school every day, but especially during holiday meals when chinaware, crystal goblets, sterling silver flatware, and linen tablecloth and napkins were used.

Every January 1, we motored to Grandpa and Grandma Pfeiffer's house in Bismarck for a bounteous meal complete with fine table appointments. Grandpa sat as sentry in his comfortable dark maroon crushed velvet chair beside the picture window in their living room. "Ma, they're here!" That was her cue to rush from the kitchen to the front door. Grandma Pfeiffer opened the door and her arms to us as she jubilantly greeted us with *"Frohes Neues Jahr"* (Happy New Year)!

Ressler's Café in Bismarck was our restaurant of choice when we had the luxury of dining out with Grandpa and Grandma Pfeiffer as a family. This experience not only was an opportunity to use our proper table manners, but also served as a treat on Mother's Day when we could try different foods that were not raised on our farm. Northern pike, halibut, and shrimp were our dining-out favorites.

The tradition of giving flowers on Mother's Day was observed by Dad, as each year he purchased a white carnation corsage for his mother and a red carnation corsage for Mom that they proudly wore to church and to the restaurant. Customarily, the white carnation was given to a mother whose mother was deceased; a red carnation was given to a mother whose mother was alive.

Jackie

IN ADDITION TO the structured learning sessions of piano and dance, many of life's lessons were discovered in an unorganized setting. We two sisters learned from our parents about integrity, honesty, morality, and work ethic, among other foundations of character.

Even as a youngster, I deduced that Dad had learned from Grandpa about the value of being kind to all and about helping those less fortunate. Janine and I watched and learned as we saw Dad carry on this tradition for the benefit of a variety of folks. There was no fanfare, no bragging; if Dad saw a family in need, he helped those less fortunate either anonymously or directly, but with discretion so as not to cause embarrassment to the receiver.

After reading through some newspaper clippings that Grandma Pfeiffer had kept, I comprehended that Grandpa had learned these values from his stepfather, Chris Wetzstein. Grandpa was age three when his father died, and Mr. Wetzstein had nurtured Grandpa's character.

At one time, I came across an article that Grandma had clipped from a newspaper that recorded Grandpa C.A. Pfeiffer's philanthropic character. (The article did not elaborate on this specific philanthropic matter.) More than likely, Grandpa would have been embarrassed by the article since he was a private, non-boastful man.

Grandpa and Grandma Pfeiffer had retired from farming near Goodrich and had moved into a home in Bismarck. Dad's A-number-one helper was Grandpa, who drove out to our farm four days a week. Janine and I often ran out to greet him as he waited for Dad to begin his day outdoors. Assuming Grandpa had brought a mini Tootsie Roll or a stick of chewing gum in his car, we excitedly asked him, "What do you have in your car, Grandpa?" He replied, "Gas." Our determined response was, "No, what do you have in your car?" He grinned and chuckled and replied, "Oh, look what I have in my pocket!" Then he turned out one pocket of his navy-blue overalls and revealed a treat for each of us.

I often worked with Grandpa on the farm. General upkeep and repairs were always needed on corrals, perimeter fences, and machinery. One summer day Dad asked me to help him and Grandpa shingle the south lean-to of the barn and the cattle shed. I was thrilled to have been asked! It would be a new experience, and it would give me a chance to be with my two favorite men at the same time. Mom was concerned about my safety and undeniably wasn't enthusiastic about that idea, though.

In spite of Mom's concern, I shinnied up the sturdy, wooden ladder and reached for the empty paint can that contained roofing nails and hammer. I put into practice Dad's teaching by example and slung my hammer precisely over each nail head. Dad stressed the importance of safety. I didn't fall off the barn roof!

Dad taught me the value of caring for one's possessions—tools, machinery, animals, buildings, and more. And he taught their proper care. For instance, when a job using a shovel had been completed, the shovel was well cleaned to prevent rust from forming due to moisture contained in the remaining debris. Likewise, metal tools that were primarily used in the growing season were put to bed for the winter with a thin grease blanket to avoid rust formation.

The integrity of wooden buildings and fences suffered in the harsh, extreme temperatures of North Dakota. Caring for wooden structures included re-nailing loose boards and applying paint often. Dad started me on my farm painting career gradually; the corral fences and farm buildings became my palette during the summers of my teen years.

When I was twelve, Grandpa thought it was time for me to learn to drive a tractor. Of course, I agreed with that idea! He started me on what was fondly known in our family as the "Little A," a red Farmall A. Driving it could be dangerous because it could "buck," meaning the front part of the tractor could pop up if the clutch was released too quickly.

I had fun driving all around the yard! Because of my experience driving the tractor, learning to drive the truck with its stick shift was an easy progression. My truck-driving ability provided Mom with more time because, as a teenager, I drove the truck on Saturdays during harvest.

Whatever the job, working with Dad or Grandpa endowed me with many too-many-to-mention skills and experiences that have helped me beyond the living-on-the-farm years!

I WAS SURROUNDED by a bounty of sensual pleasures as I stood on the prairie. Likewise, Jackie and Janine were immersed within a variety of lessons learned outside the schoolhouse walls. The results of those lessons were infused into their characters. It was good!

Chapter 16

Our Last Words

GROWING UP on the vast prairie could have instilled a feeling of isolation within the souls of us sisters. There are stories of other rural North Dakotans whose childhoods reflected that feeling. However, we never experienced the reality of remoteness. Perhaps it was our proximity to the capital city and the opportunities it presented to us. Perhaps it was the fact that our parents gave us a peek into a world beyond farm life while at the same time offering emotional and physical shelter and security within our environment.

Our parents exhibited security through verbal encouragement and by giving us a home where patience and understanding were displayed and where hugs and kisses comforted.

At times, a child's nighttime imagination can cause fright. However, Mom and Dad's bedtime ritual warded off that possible feeling. They had their own unique methods of tucking us into bed at night. Prayers said and stories read with Mom prefaced securing bed covers around us. With covers tucked under our chins, Mom's method was to place a hand on each side of our necks and give a gentle tuck. She would leave us with "Night, night, sleep tight. Don't let the bedbugs bite."

Dad expanded on Mom's method and cozily tucked the covers from shoulders to toes. Even though our bedrooms were heated by the forced air from the basement coal furnace, the heat coming through the tiny register never seemed to rise to bed level. The bedtime tucks not only comfortably warded off the chill of the night but also provided safe and loving contentment and security as the night came upon us.

As little girls sitting on Dad's lap, we were surrounded by his arms and felt securely safe and loved.

Upon reflection on the journey of our lives in rural America during the 1950s, the words inscribed on these pages opened our eyes to the blessed gift of being the daughters of Jack and Eudora Pfeiffer. This writing experience further deepened the understanding of our incredible cherished legacy.

As
We
Part

FOR A PERIOD OF TIME in history, I stood tall and notably served my role in delivering water to the Pfeiffer family farm. Likewise, I humbly observed the Pfeiffers and the Menoken community as they faced the difficulties and rewards of life on the challenging North Dakota prairie.

Each calendar day, the family's life's journey saw many twists and turns. Four years of secondary education at Bismarck High School were exchanged for maroon mortar boards and gold-sealed diplomas—Jackie, class of 1965 and Janine, class of 1968.

From my vantage point, I saw Jack and Eudora gradually sport strands of gray hair, along with an increased number of wrinkles. However, this team still had plenty of future farming years in their blood, which was a good thing! College tuition had to be paid!

North Dakota State University became The Sisters' home of higher learning. Each sister's nine-year 4-H alumna status played a key role in the selection of her chosen major field of study. And professors in the College of Home Economics had the opportunity to strengthen the young ladies' previously acquired knowledge.

When I introduced myself and the Pfeiffers, I mentioned that Jackie and Janine were strikingly similar yet uniquely different in their characters. Although both girls majored in home economics education, Jackie chose a study emphasis in foods and the social sciences with graduate study later. On the other hand, with Janine's passion for livestock, her areas of emphasis were in animal science and foods.

Jackie taught home economics and family living at Ashley High School, where she met Enderlin native and teacher of chemistry, physics, and general science, Bob McGregor. They soon married and satisfied their shared desire to live and teach on The Last Frontier at Sitka, Alaska. For seventeen years, Jackie continued her love of dance as a member of the New Archangel Dancers, a Russian folk-dance group that performed for thousands of Alaskan cruise ship visitors.

Two beautiful daughters, Kinsey and Kaali, joined their family. Both daughters married wisely; they and their spouses continued to value the Pfeiffer endorsement of the importance of education by earning advanced university degrees. The couples gifted Jackie and Bob with four "joys"—three boys and one girl.

Jackie and Bob are retired, wear professional volunteer hats, and enjoy the outdoor sporting opportunities in the Colville, Washington, area. In Bob, Jackie found a partner who also wanted to "climb to the top of the windmill" to view a world beyond the farm!

After Janine finished college, she took the professional role of home economist for Otter Tail Power Company, Fergus Falls, Minnesota—but only for a year. She had met her kindred spirit while they were members of their respective collegiate livestock judging teams. Iowa native Fred Knop married our North Dakota farm girl and whisked her away to his family farm near Atlantic, Iowa.

Two gracious daughters, Brittney and Louise, blessed their family. The "apple didn't fall far from the tree" as the four Knops were united in their love for nurturing and showing livestock. Janine lived her childhood dream! During the girls' combined twelve-year tenure in 4-H and FFA, their home-raised market lambs garnered championships at many major livestock shows across the United States. This passion ignited the beginning of the Knops' sheep-genetics business, which is recognized nationwide and continues to this day.

Both Janine and Fred are retired from farming and carry on with their mobile gourmet coffee cart business and Janine's dessert-baking business, Miss NiNi's Fine Desserts. Completing their family are loving sons-in-law and grandchildren.

I NO LONGER STAND TALL on the North Dakota prairie, but personal memories, just like the wind, continue forever. With advancing years, my functional service declined; my watchful eye observed with only fading clarity.

Escorted by fond echoes of the past, I witnessed the family's patriarch and matriarch as they eased into life's waning years. Jack and Eudora gradually retired from active farming. Their travels to destinations beyond the horizon found fulfilling moments with their family as they watched Jackie and Janine carve new chapters into their destinies while staying true to the respected virtues of their childhood.

Jack and Eudora's "until death do us part" came to pass in the 1980s. Until that time, they lived in the house they had built on their farm in the Menoken community. The family's indelible rural legacy is encased within the cover of this book. Their productive slice of North Dakota prairie—those acres over which I stood observing their family life and the Menoken community—the land they lovingly stewarded with every inch of their being, remains in the Pfeiffer family today.

The Pfeiffer farmstead

"There are only two lasting bequests
we can hope to give our children.
One of these is roots,
the other, wings."

—*Johann Wolfgang von Goethe*

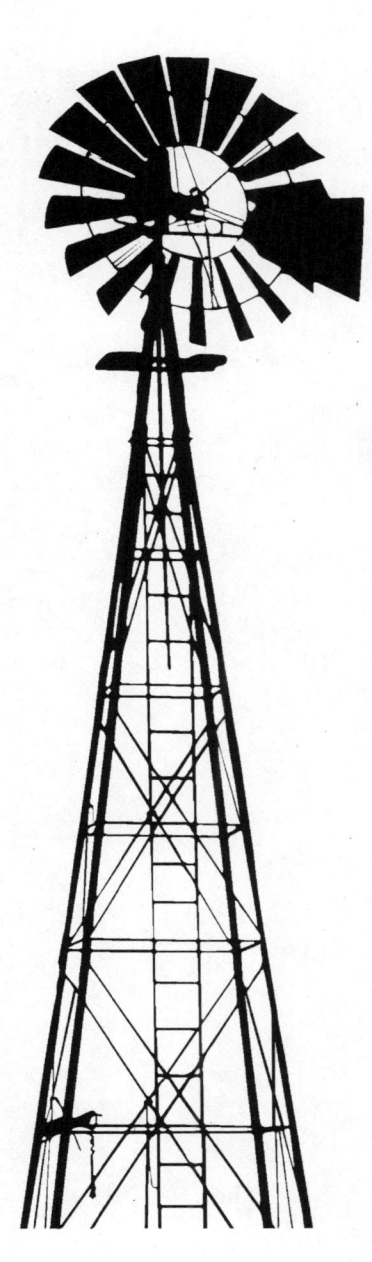

Recipes

Old-Fashioned Date Balls

Gladys Goehring

Menoken, North Dakota

Ingredients:
- 2 large eggs
- 1-1/2 c. dates, finely chopped
- 1 c. sugar
- 5 tbsp. butter
- 2-1/2 c. crispy rice cereal
- 1 tsp. vanilla
- 1/2 c. chopped English walnuts
- 1/2 c. shredded coconut
- Additional 1–2 c. shredded coconut

Directions:
In a bowl, beat eggs. Stir in dates and sugar. Melt butter in skillet. Add eggs, dates, and sugar. Cool until thick. Add crispy rice cereal, vanilla, English walnuts, and 1/2 c. coconut. Mix and cool. Form into teaspoon-size balls and roll in remaining coconut. Keep refrigerated due to cooked egg mixture. Yields about 5 dozen.

Devil's Food Cake

Peggy Owen & Maureen Kershaw

Menoken, North Dakota

Ingredients:
- 1/2 c. butter or bacon fryings
- 2 c. sugar
- 2 eggs
- 1/2 tsp. salt
- 1/2 c. sour milk
- 2 tsp. baking soda
- 2-1/2 c. flour
- 2 tsp. vanilla
- 1/2 c. cocoa
- 1 c. boiling water

Directions:

Grease and flour sides and bottom of 9 x 13-inch cake pan. Cream sugar and butter; add eggs—beat well. Add salt, sour milk, and vanilla. Dissolve cocoa in hot water. Cool. Add soda to cocoa and water mixture. Add to other ingredients; add flour. Bake at 375° F until done (about 35 minutes). Yields 1 cake.

Coffee-Toffee Torte

Mom

Ingredients:
- 1 – 3.4-oz. package chocolate pudding (cook and serve)
- 1-1/2 tbsp. instant coffee
- 1-1/3 c. milk
- 1 c. heavy cream, whipped
- 1 angel food cake
- 1 – 1.4-oz. toffee candy such as Heath bar, crushed into medium-size pieces

Directions:

Mix coffee and pudding in saucepan. Prepare according to package directions but using only the amount of milk listed in this recipe. Chill.

Beat chilled pudding mixture until smooth; fold in one-half of the whipped cream. Split angel food cake into three layers. Spread half of pudding mix between layers. For the frosting, fold remaining whipped cream into the remaining pudding mix. Frost sides and top of cake. Sprinkle with crushed toffee bars. Chill. Yields 12 servings.

Baked Potato Candy (Depression Candy)

Marge Perkins

Menoken, North Dakota

Ingredients:

1 medium-size baked potato, warm
1/2 c. sifted powdered sugar
Additional sifted powdered sugar to make a stiff dough
6–12 ounces semisweet chocolate chips, melted
Flavoring options: 1 tsp. vanilla plus 1/4 c. finely chopped English walnuts, OR a few drops of mint flavoring plus 1 drop of green food coloring, OR a few drops of maraschino cherry juice plus 2 tbsp. well-drained, finely chopped maraschino cherries. (Amounts added will vary depending on the intensity of flavor desired.)

Directions:

Remove baked potato pulp from skin with a fork or a potato masher; add 1/2 c. sifted powdered sugar; mix until a smooth paste forms. Add chosen flavoring. Keep adding powdered sugar until stiff dough forms. Shape into small balls or a long roll. Refrigerate until set. Coat with melted chocolate chips. To slice roll, dip thin sharp knife in hot water. Cut slices about 1/4 inch thick. Yield varies.

Peanut Butter Fudge
Mom

Ingredients:
- 1 c. brown sugar, packed
- 1 c. sugar
- 1 c. peanut butter
- 1 c. sour cream
- 1/8 tsp. salt
- 1/2 tsp. vanilla

Directions:

Mix sugars, salt, and cream into large sturdy saucepan. Boil without stirring to soft ball stage (235°–245° F). Cool to lukewarm. Beat until creamy. Fold in peanut butter. Pour into 8-inch square pan which has been buttered or lined with wax paper. Cool and cut into squares. Yields about 2 pounds.

Speedy Creamy Fudge
Mom

Ingredients:
1 – 14-oz. package (2-1/3 c.) semisweet chocolate chips
1-1/3 c. (15-oz. can) sweetened condensed milk
1 tsp. vanilla
1 c. chopped English walnuts

Directions:
Melt chocolate in top of double boiler. Add sweetened condensed milk and stir until well blended. Remove from heat. Add vanilla and walnuts. Pour into 8-inch square pan which has been buttered or lined with wax paper. Chill for a few hours. When firm, cut into squares. Yields about 2 pounds.

Divinity
Mom

Ingredients:
- 1-2/3 c. sugar
- 2/3 c. light corn syrup
- 1/2 c. water (use 1 tbsp. less on humid days)
- 2 large egg whites, room temperature
- 1 tsp. vanilla
- 2/3 c. broken English walnuts

Directions:
Line three baking pans (15 x 10 x 1-inch) with wax paper. In heavy saucepan, stir sugar, corn syrup, and water over low heat until sugar is dissolved. Cook without stirring to 252°–266° F on candy thermometer (or until a small amount of mixture dropped into very cold water forms a hard ball).

In mixing bowl, beat egg whites until stiff peaks form. Continue beating while pouring hot syrup in a thin stream into egg whites. Add vanilla; beat until mixture holds its shape and becomes slightly dull. Immediately fold in nuts. Drop mixture from tip of buttered spoon onto wax paper-lined baking pans. Let stand at room temperature until dry to touch. Yields about 4 dozen.

Russian Tea Cakes
Mom

Ingredients:
- 1 c. soft butter
- 1/2 c. confectioners' sugar
- 1 tsp. vanilla
- 2-1/4 c. flour
- 3/4 tsp. salt
- 3/4 c. finely chopped English walnuts or pecans
- Additional confectioners' sugar

Directions:

In large bowl cream butter and sugar until light and fluffy, two minutes. Blend in vanilla. Set aside. In smaller bowl combine flour and salt; gradually add to creamed mixture. Stir in nuts. Cover and refrigerate 1–2 hours.

Preheat oven at 350° F. Roll dough into 1-inch balls. Place 2 inches apart on a parchment-lined ungreased baking sheet. Bake for 12–13 minutes. Roll in confectioners' sugar while still warm. Cool on wire rack. Yields about 4 dozen.

Chinese Chews
Mom

Ingredients:
    1 – 10-oz. bag crispy chow mein noodles
    1 – 12-oz. package chocolate chips
    1 – 12-oz. package butterscotch chips
    1 c. Spanish peanuts

Directions:
Melt chocolate and butterscotch chips in double boiler. Remove from heat. Stir in chow mein noodles and Spanish peanuts. Drop from a teaspoon onto a cookie sheet. Cool. Yields 3–4 dozen.

Seven-Layer Bars
Mom

Ingredients:
- 1/2 c. butter, melted
- 1-1/2 c. graham cracker crumbs
- 1 – 14-oz. can sweetened condensed milk
- 1 c. semisweet chocolate chips
- 1 c. butterscotch chips
- 1-1/3 c. flaked coconut
- 1 c. chopped nuts

Directions:
Preheat oven to 350° F (325° F for glass dish). Spray a 9 x 13-inch baking pan with non-stick spray. Combine graham cracker crumbs and butter. Press into bottom of prepared pan. Drizzle sweetened condensed milk over crumb mixture. Layer evenly with chocolate chips, butterscotch chips, coconut, and nuts. Press down firmly with a fork. Bake at 350° F for 25 minutes or until lightly browned. Cool. Cut into rectangular bars. Yields 3 dozen.

Oatmeal Crispies
Mom

Ingredients:
- 1 c. shortening (Crisco)
- 1 c. brown sugar, packed
- 1 c. sugar
- 2 large eggs
- 1 tsp. vanilla
- 1-1/2 c. all-purpose flour
- 1 tsp. salt
- 1 tsp. baking soda
- 3 c. quick oats
- 1/2 c. finely chopped pecans

Directions:

In a large mixing bowl, cream shortening with both sugars until well combined.

In a separate bowl, beat eggs together. Add vanilla and stir to combine. Add to the shortening/sugar mixture and mix well.

In a separate bowl combine the flour, salt, and baking soda. Mix carefully into the egg/shortening mixture until well combined. Now add the quick oats and mix well again. Finally add the finely chopped pecans and mix well to combine.

Pack the dough into metal orange juice cans. Let sit until dough is firm. Slice cookies 1/8-inch thick and place onto cookie sheet. Or divide the dough in half and place each half of the dough onto a sheet of wax paper. Roll the dough into a log and then wrap it tightly in the wax paper. Either chill or freeze the dough until later, or go ahead and slice the dough evenly into cookie rounds.

Place the slices on a cookie sheet and bake at 350° F for 10 minutes until they are golden brown. Yields about 24 cookies.

About the Authors

World traveler and adventurer **Jackie Pfeiffer McGregor** lives near Colville, Washington, with her husband, Bob. The two retirees spend much of their time volunteering and enjoying the outdoor activities of hiking and kayaking in northeastern Washington.

Entrepreneur **Janine Pfeiffer Knop** and her husband, Fred, farm together near Atlantic, Iowa, where they also breed and raise award-winning sheep. Many of her days start in the kitchen, the hub of her local and online business, Miss NiNi's Fine Desserts.